PHILOSOPHY

PHILOSOPHY

Edward Craig

A BRIEF INSIGHT

STERLING

New York / London
www.sterlingpublishing.com

STERLING and the distinctive Sterling logo are registered trademarks of
Sterling Publishing Co., Inc.

Library of Congress Cataloging-in-Publication Data Available

10 9 8 7 6 5 4 3 2 1

Published by Sterling Publishing Co., Inc.
387 Park Avenue South, New York, NY 10016

Published by arrangement with Oxford University Press, Inc.

Copyright © 2002 Edward Craig
Illustrated edition published in 2009 by Sterling Publishing Co., Inc.
Additional text © 2009 Sterling Publishing Co., Inc.

Distributed in Canada by Sterling Publishing
c/o Canadian Manda Group, 165 Dufferin Street
Toronto, Ontario, Canada M6K 3H6

Book design and layout: The DesignWorks Group

Please see picture credits on page 185 for image copyright information.

Manufactured in the United States of America
All rights reserved

Sterling ISBN 978-1-4027-6877-4

For information about custom editions, special sales, premium and
corporate purchases, please contact Sterling Special Sales
Department at 800-805-5489 or specialsales@sterlingpublishing.com.

Frontispiece: *The Discourse; A Chat* (oil on panel) by Sir Lawrence Alma-Tadema (1836–1912)

CONTENTS

•

ONE

Philosophy: An Introduction

•

ANYONE READING THIS BOOK is to some extent a philosopher already. Nearly all of us are, because we have some kind of values by which we live our lives (or like to think we do, or feel uncomfortable when we don't). And most of us favor some very general picture of what the world is like. Perhaps we think there's a god who made it all, including us; or, on the contrary, we think it's all a matter of chance and natural selection. Perhaps we believe that people have immortal, nonmaterial parts called souls or spirits; or, quite the opposite, that we are just complicated arrangements of matter that gradually fall to bits after we die. So most of us, even those who don't *think about it* at all, have something like answers to the two basic philosophical questions, namely: what should we do? and, what is there? And there's a third basic question, to which again most of us have some kind of an answer, which kicks in the moment we get self-conscious about either of

Antonio da Trento, *The Philosopher*, chiaroscuro woodcut (between 1530 and 1550).

the first two questions, namely: how do we know, or if we don't know how should we set about finding out—use our eyes, think, consult an oracle, ask a scientist? Philosophy, thought of as a subject that you can study, be ignorant of, get better at, even be an expert on, simply means being rather more reflective about some of these questions and their interrelations, learning what has already been said about them and why.

Most of us hold a general view of what the world is like—some favoring the idea of a creator-god, others believing in a random and natural selection; some holding that people are simply complicated compilations of matter, others believing that people have nonmaterial spirits or souls, as depicted in *The Spirit's Flight*, a hand-colored 1893 Currier & Ives lithograph, where an angel hovers above two spirits.

In fact philosophy is extremely hard to avoid, even with a conscious effort. Consider someone who rejects it, telling us that "philosophy is useless." For a start, they are evidently measuring it against some system of values. Secondly, the moment they are prepared to say, however briefly and dogmatically, why it is useless, they will be talking about the ineffectuality of certain types of thought, or of human beings' incapacity to deal with certain types of question. And then instead of rejecting philosophy they will have become another voice *within* it—a skeptical voice, admittedly, but then philosophy has never been short of skeptical voices, from the earliest times to the present day. We shall meet some of them in Chapter 6.

If they take the second of those lines, they may also be implying that making the discovery that human beings just can't cope with certain kinds of question, and making that discovery *for yourself*—and actually *making it*, rather than just lazily assuming that you know it already—isn't a valuable experience, or is an experience without effects. Surely that cannot be true? Imagine how different the world would have been if we were all convinced that human beings just aren't up to answering any questions about the nature or even existence of a god, in other words, if all human beings were religious agnostics. Imagine how different it would have been if we were all convinced that there was no answer to the question of what legitimates the political authority that states habitually exercise over their members, in other words, if none of us believed that there was any good answer to the anarchist. It may well be controversial whether the differences would have been for the good, or for the bad, or whether in fact they wouldn't have mattered as much as you might at first think; but that there would have been differences, and very big ones, is surely beyond question. That how people think alters things, and that how lots of people think alters things for nearly everyone, is undeniable. A more sensible objection to philosophy than that it is ineffectual is pretty much the opposite: that it is *too dangerous*. (Nietzsche—see Chapter 7—called a philosopher "a terrible explosive from which nothing is safe," though he didn't mean that as an objection.) But what this usually means is that any philosophy is dangerous *except the speaker's own*, and what it amounts to is fear of what might happen if things change.

It might occur to you that perhaps there are people who don't even think it worthwhile to enter into this discussion at all, however briefly, not even to support the skeptical stance that I have just mentioned. And you would be right, but that doesn't mean to say that they don't have a philosophy. Far from it. It may mean that they are not prepared to "philosophize"—to state their views and argue for them or discourse upon them. But it doesn't mean that they have no abiding values, nothing which they systematically regard as worthwhile. They might think, for instance, that real expertise at *doing* something is more desirable than any amount of theoretical knowledge. Their ideal would not so much be

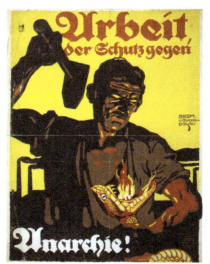

How lots of people think alters things for nearly everybody: imagine if everyone was convinced that there was no good answer to the anarchist. This 1875 German poster shows an early response to the threat of anarchy: "Work, the protection against anarchy."

While there are people who do not think it worthwhile to engage in the discussion of philosophy, this does not mean that they do not have any abiding values. For example, much Zen Buddhist thought espouses the idea that real expertise at *doing* something—training oneself to perform an activity instinctively—is more valuable than any amount of philosophical knowledge. Chinese Zen Buddhist monk Wuzhun Shifan, who practiced during the late Song dynasty, is shown here in a detail from a silk hand scroll.

insight into the nature of reality as the capacity to become one with it in the execution of some particular activity, to have trained oneself to do something without conscious effort as if by a perfectly honed natural instinct. I am not just making these people up: a lot of Zen Buddhist thought, or perhaps I should say Zen Buddhist practice, leans strongly in this direction. And this ideal, of aiming at a certain kind of thoughtlessness, was the outcome of a great deal of previous thinking.

If philosophy is so close to us, why do so many people think that it is something very abstruse and rather weird? It isn't that they are simply wrong: some philosophy *is* abstruse and weird, and a lot of the best philosophy is likely to *seem* abstruse or weird at first. That's because the best philosophy doesn't just come up with a few new facts that we can simply add to our stock of information, or a few new maxims to extend our list of dos and don'ts, but embodies a picture of the world and/or a set of values; and unless these happen to be yours already (remember that in a vague and unreflective way we all have them) it is bound to seem very peculiar—if it doesn't seem peculiar you haven't understood it.

Good philosophy expands your imagination. Some philosophy is close to us, whoever we are. Then of course some is further away, and some is further still, and some is very alien indeed. It would be disappointing if that were not so, because it would imply that human beings are intellectually rather monotonous. But there's no need to start at the deep end; we start at the shallow end, where (as I've said) we are all standing in the water already. Do remember, however (here the analogy with the swimming pool leaves me in the lurch, the way analogies often do), that this doesn't necessarily mean that we are all standing in the same place: what is shallow and familiar, and what is deep and weird, may depend on where you got in, and when.

Both Hindus and Buddhists believe that the purpose of philosophy is the relief of human suffering through a cycle of death and rebirth in which one's future form depends on one's past actions. A depiction of this cycle is shown here in a Tibetan Buddhist bhavachakra, or wheel of becoming.

Followers of Epicureanism
espoused the belief that one's
purpose in life was to seek modest
pleasures while avoiding fear
and pain. The school of thought
was founded by ancient Greek
philosopher Epicurus (341–270
BCE), shown here in a copy of a
lost original from the late third or
early second century BCE.

We may be standing in the water, but why try to swim? In other words, what is philosophy for? There is far too much philosophy, composed under far too wide a range of conditions, for there to be a general answer to that question. But it can certainly be said that a great deal of philosophy has been intended as (understanding the words very broadly) a means to salvation, though what we are to understand by salvation, and salvation from what, has varied as widely as the philosophies themselves. A Buddhist will tell you that the purpose of philosophy is the relief of human suffering and the attainment of "enlightenment"; a Hindu will say something similar, if in slightly different terminology; both will speak of escape from a supposed cycle of death and rebirth in which one's moral deserts determine one's future forms. An Epicurean (if you can find one nowadays) will pooh-pooh all the stuff about rebirth, but offer you a recipe for maximizing pleasure and minimizing suffering in this your one and only life.

Not all philosophy has sprung out of a need for a comprehensive way of living and dying. But most of the philosophy that has lasted has arisen from some pressing motivation or deeply felt belief—seeking truth and wisdom purely for their own sakes may be a nice idea, but history suggests that a nice idea is pretty much all it is. Thus classical Indian philosophy represents the internal struggle between the schools of Hinduism, and between them all and the Buddhists, for intellectual supremacy; the battle for the preferred balance between human reason and scriptural revelation has been fought in many cultures, and in some is still going on; Thomas Hobbes's famous political theory (we shall be seeing more of it later) tries to teach us the lessons he felt had to be learned in the aftermath of the English Civil War; Descartes and many of his contemporaries wanted medieval views, rooted nearly two thousand years back in the work of Aristotle, to move aside and make room for a modern conception of science; Kant sought to advance the autonomy of the individual in the face of illiberal and autocratic regimes, Marx to liberate the working classes from poverty and drudgery, feminists of all epochs to improve the status of women. None of these people were just solving little puzzles (though they did sometimes have to solve little puzzles on the way); they entered into debate in order to change the course of civilization.

The reader will notice that I haven't made any attempt to define philosophy, but have just implied that it is an extremely broad term covering a very wide range of intellectual activities. Some think that nothing is to be gained from trying to define it. I can sympathize with that thought, since most attempts strike me as much too restrictive, and therefore harmful rather than helpful insofar as they have any effect at all. But I will at least have a shot at saying what philosophy is; whether what I have to offer counts as a definition or not is something about which we needn't, indeed positively shouldn't, bother too much.

Once, a very long time ago, our ancestors were animals, and simply did whatever came naturally without noticing that that was what they were doing, or indeed without noticing that *they* were doing anything at all. Then, somehow, they acquired the capacities to ask *why* things happen (as opposed to just registering that they do), and to look at themselves and their actions. That is not as big a jump as may at first sight appear. Starting to ask why things happen is in the first place only a matter of becoming a little more conscious of aspects of one's own behavior. A hunting animal that follows a scent is acting as if aware that the scent is there because its prey has recently passed that way—and it is because that really is why the scent is there that it often succeeds in its hunt. Knowledge of this sort of connection can be very useful: it tells us what to expect. Furthermore, to know that A happens because B happened may improve your control over things: in some cases B will be something that you can bring about, or prevent—which will be very useful if A is something you want, or want to avoid. Many of these connections animals, humans included, follow naturally and unconsciously. And the practice, once one is aware of it, can valuably be extended by consciously raising such questions in cases where we do not have conveniently built-in answers.

Hand-colored Currier & Ives lithograph from 1850–1900 of an elk escaping from a pack of wolves.

There could be no guarantee, however, that this generally valuable tendency would always pay off, let alone always pay off quickly. Asking why fruit falls off a branch pretty soon leads one to shake the tree. Asking why it rains, or why it doesn't rain, takes us into a different league, especially when the real motive underlying the question is whether we can influence whether it rains or not. Often we can influence events, and it may well pay to develop the habit of asking, when things (a hunting expedition, for example) have gone wrong, whether that was because we failed in our part of the performance, as opposed to being defeated by matters beyond our control. That same useful habit might have generated the thought that a drought is to some extent due to a failure of ours—and now what failure, what have we done wrong? And then an idea might crop up which served us well in our infancy: there are parents, who do things for us that we can't do ourselves, but only if we've been good and they aren't cross with us. Might there be beings that decide whether the rain falls, and shouldn't we be trying to get on the right side of them?

That is all it would take for human beings to be launched into the investigation of nature and belief in the supernatural. So as their mental capacities developed, our ancestors found their power increasing; but they also found themselves confronted by options and mysteries—life raised a host of questions, where previously it had simply been lived, unquestioningly. It is just as well that all this happened gradually, but even so it was the biggest shock the species has ever encountered. Some people, thinking more in intellectual than biological terms, might like to say that it was what made us human at all.

Think of philosophy as the sound of humanity trying to recover from this crisis. Thinking of it like that will protect you from certain

Though there is no documented evidence that they work, rain dances—ceremonial rites to invoke rain and ensure the safety of the harvest—have been a part of the custom of many cultures, from ancient Egyptian to Native American to twentieth-century Balkans. This photograph, taken around 1920, shows Chief Turtle giving his interpretation of the Native Americans' storm dance, just before the rain came down in torrents, at the Indian celebration in Two Medicine Valley, Glacier National Park, Montana.

common misapprehensions. One is that philosophy is a rather narrow operation that occurs only in universities, or (less absurdly) only in particular epochs or particular cultures; another, related to the first, is that it is something of an intellectual game, answering to no very deep need. On the positive side, it may lead you to expect that the history of philosophy is likely to contain some fascinating episodes, as indeed it does, and it certainly adds to the excitement if we bear in mind that view of what is really going on. Can reeling *Homo sapiens* think his way back to the vertical? We have no good reason to answer that question either way, yes or no. Are we even sure that we know where the vertical is? That's the kind of open-ended adventure we are stuck with, like it or not.

But isn't that just too broad? Surely philosophy doesn't include everything that that account of it implies? Well, in the first place, it will do us less harm to err on the broad side than the narrow. And in the second place, the scope of the word *philosophy* has itself varied considerably through history, not to mention the fact that there has probably never been a time at which it meant the same thing to everyone. Recently something rather strange has happened to it. On the one hand it has become so broad as to be close to meaningless, as when almost every commercial organization speaks of itself as having a philosophy—usually meaning a policy. On the other hand it has become very narrow. A major factor here has been the development of the natural sciences. It has often been remarked that when an area of inquiry begins to find its feet as a discipline, with clearly agreed methods and a clearly agreed body of knowledge, fairly soon it separates off from what has up to then been known as philosophy and goes its own way, as for instance physics, chemistry, astronomy, psychology. So the range of questions considered by people who think of themselves as philosophers shrinks; and furthermore, philosophy tends to be left in charge of those questions which we are not sure how best to formulate, those inquiries we are not sure how best to set about.

This multiplication of thriving disciplines inevitably brings another factor into play, namely, specialization within universities, and creates the opportunity to think of philosophy yet more narrowly. University philosophy departments are mostly quite small. In consequence, so is the range of their expertise, which tends to cluster around current (sometimes also local) academic fashion—it must do, since it is normally they who make it. Besides, undergraduate courses are, for obvious reasons, quite short, and therefore have to be selective on pain of gross superficiality. So the natural assumption that philosophy is what university philosophy departments teach, though I certainly wouldn't call it false, is restrictive and misleading, and ought to be avoided.

This book is an introduction to philosophy. But, as I hope is now becoming clear, I can't exactly *introduce* you to philosophy, because you are already there. Nor can I exactly introduce you to *philosophy*, because there is far too much of it. No more could I "show you London." I could show you a few bits of it, perhaps mention a handful of other main attractions, and leave you on your own with a street map and some information about other guided tours. That's pretty much what I propose to do for philosophy.

At the beginning of this chapter I spoke of three philosophical questions, though they might better have been called three types or classes of question. Chapters 2–4 introduce, from a classic text, an example of each type. By progressing from very familiar ways of thinking in the first to something most readers will find altogether stranger in the third, they also

University undergraduate courses in philosophy have to be highly selective in what they teach—otherwise they would become very superficial. So to think of philosophy as just what is taught in university philosophy departments would be restrictive and misleading. This late-fourteenth-century parchment from *Liber ethicorum des Henricus de Alemannia* (Henricus de Alemannia's book of moral philosophy) shows Laurentius de Voltolina's *Henricus de Alemannia in Front of His Pupils*.

illustrate (though not by any means in its full extent) another theme of this introduction: the range of novelty to be encountered in philosophy. I have also harped on somewhat about the difficulty of avoiding being philosophical. If that is so, we should expect to find some kind of philosophy more or less wherever we look. As if to confirm that, our first example comes from Greece and the fourth century BCE, our second from eighteenth-century Scotland, and our third from India, written by an unknown Buddhist at an unknown date probably between 100 BCE and 100 CE.

All three of these texts should be fairly easy to obtain, especially the first two (see the bibliography). This book can perfectly well be read without them, but there are good reasons to read them yourself alongside it if that is possible. One is to be able to enjoy the writing. Much philosophy is well written, and it is strongly recommended to enjoy the writing as well as the views and the arguments. But the main reason is that it will enable you to *join in* if you want to. Remember that this is not a completely foreign country: you are to some extent already a philosopher, and your ordinary native intelligence has a work permit here—you don't need to go through any esoteric training to get a license to think. So don't be afraid, as you read, to start asking questions and forming provisional conclusions. But notice, *provisional*. Whatever you do, don't get hooked up on that laziest, most complacent of sayings, that "everyone has a right to their own opinion." Acquiring rights isn't that simple. Rather, keep in mind the wry comment of George Berkeley (1685–1753): "Few men think, yet all will have opinions." If true, that's a pity; for one thing, the thinking is part of the fun.

Finally, please read slowly. This is a short book about a very long subject. I have tried to pack a lot in.

TWO

What Should I Do?
Plato's *Crito*

●

PLATO, WHO WAS BORN in or around 427 BCE and died in 347, was not the first important philosopher of ancient Greek civilization, but he is the first from whom a substantial body of complete works has come down to us. In the Indian tradition, the Vedas and many of the Upanishads are earlier; but of their authors, and how they were composed, we know next to nothing. The Buddha predated Plato, though by just how much is a matter of scholarly disagreement; but the earliest surviving accounts of his life and thought were written down some hundreds of years after his death. In China, Confucius also predated Plato (he was born in the middle of the previous century); again, we have nothing known to have been written by him—the famous *Analects* are a later compilation.

The Academy of Athens, as pictured on the Greek ten-drachma banknote from 1940.

: form of dialogues. Mostly they are quick-
il in style, though sometimes the protago-
extended speeches. There are two dozen or
Plato, and a handful more that may be. Of
up two are much longer than the others, and
s consisting of sequences of dialogues. (They
oth devoted to the search for the ideal political
constitution.) So there s plenty of Plato to read, and most of it is fairly
easy to obtain, in translation in relatively inexpensive editions. As regards
degree of difficulty, the range is wide. At one end we have a number of
dialogues comparable to the one we shall shortly
be taking a close look at. At the other are
works like *The Sophist*, capable at times
of making the most experienced readers
scratch their heads and look blank.

A near constant feature of Plato's
dialogues is the presence of Socrates,
usually though not always as the leader
of the discussion. Since the dialogue
called *Crito* is not only conducted
by Socrates but also concerns what
he, personally, should do in a certain predicament in which he finds
himself, we need to know a little
about him and how he got into the
situation he is in when the dialogue
opens—namely in prison in Athens
awaiting imminent execution.

This marble bust of Socrates, from the
Quintili Villa on the Via Appia, is a Roman
copy after a Greek original from the fourth
century BCE.

Socrates lived from 469 to 399 BCE. He was clearly a charismatic figure, with a somewhat eccentric lifestyle. Accepting the poverty it entailed, he appears to have spent all his time in unpaid discussion with whomever would join with him, which included many of the better-off, hence more leisured, young men of Athens. These included Plato, whose admiration for Socrates motivated the career and writings which immortalized both of them.

Not all our evidence about Socrates' thought comes to us through Plato, but by far the greater part of it does, so it is no easy matter to distinguish clearly between their views. Little doubt that Plato was sometimes trying to portray the historical Socrates; little doubt that he was sometimes using the figure of Socrates as a literary device to convey his own philosophy. Where to draw the line isn't always obvious, but scholars seem now broadly agreed that the real Socrates concentrated on ethical questions about justice and virtue ("How should I live?" is sometimes called "the Socratic question"); and that he constantly probed whether his fellow Athenians really understood what was involved in these matters anything like as well as they claimed to. Nor was he always sure that he understood it himself—but then he didn't claim to.

That sounds like a pretty reliable way of making enemies, so this account of Socrates' activities fits in well enough with the next episode: three citizens, surely acting as the public tip of a hostile iceberg, brought a prosecution against him on a charge of corrupting the youth of Athens. By a small majority he was found guilty, and condemned to death. In *The Apology of Socrates* you can read Plato's version of the (totally unapologetic) speeches he made at his trial, one in his own defense, one after the verdict, one after the sentence.

Socrates was not executed straight away. At the time of his trial a ceremonial period was beginning, which would end only when an official ship returned to Athens from the island of Delos. This had religious significance, and no executions could take place while the ship was away. So Socrates had to spend this time in prison—long enough for his friends to set up a routine of visiting him, get to know the guards, and form a plan of action. With time running out, it falls to Crito to put this plan to Socrates: they propose to bribe the guards; Socrates can escape from Athens and go somewhere else, maybe to Thessaly, where Crito has friends who will offer hospitality and protection.

The dialogue *Crito* is Plato's account of their discussion and Socrates' response. Considering that this text is twenty-four hundred years old, one of the most surprising things about it is that it is

In this eighteenth-century engraving by L. P. Boitard, Socrates stands before a seated group with a figure representing truth behind them on a pedestal.

not more surprising. You may not agree with everything Socrates says—for instance, many readers will feel that his view of the claims that the state can properly make on the individual are exaggerated—but virtually all the points made will be perfectly familiar to anyone who has ever had to think about a difficult decision. When Plato writes about love we are aware that his perspective differs from ours; when we read him on cosmology we are back in a completely different age; but this discussion of a specific ethical question, "What should I do in this case?," could almost have occurred yesterday. I said in Chapter 1 that we were all to some extent philosophers, and that therefore some philosophy would feel very near home. Here is an example—from ancient Greece.

Just one word before we start. There is a standard method for referring to passages in Plato's texts, one that works whichever edition and translation you are using. It actually goes back to the pagination of a Renaissance edition published in 1578, and is known as Stephanus numbering (from the Latin name of the editor, Henri Estienne). Any modern edition of Plato will show it, either in the margin, or at the top of the page. I shall be using it throughout this chapter.

The first page or so (43a–44b) sets the scene. Crito mentions that he is well in with the warder. Socrates says that at his age you shouldn't complain too much about having to die. But then Crito opens his campaign of persuasion. He starts—as one well might—by telling Socrates how much his friends value him, and then implies that Socrates might care to return the compliment: his friends' reputation is at stake—if he stays in prison and dies people will think that they weren't prepared to go to the expense of buying his escape.

process of dividing into pages

During the Middle Ages Arabic scholars played a vital role in preserving the works of the ancient Greek philosophers and transmitting them to Western Europe. Socrates and two pupils are shown here in an Arabic manuscript from the early thirteenth century.

Now a lot of very different points are raised very quickly (and left half dealt with—*Crito* is not written like a well-constructed lecture, but much more like a real conversation). Socrates responds by saying that one shouldn't bother about what "people" think; the opinion that should matter to us is that of reasonable people with a clear view of the facts. "We can't afford to take that line," says Crito; "majority opinion is too powerful." "On the contrary," Socrates replies, "as regards what really matters the majority don't have much power at all." And what really matters, apparently, is whether one is wise or foolish (44d).

I suspect that this idea will strike many readers as a rather strange one. What does Socrates mean by wisdom, that it should be the only thing that really matters? We should keep that question in mind, and keep an eye open for anything later in the dialogue that might shed light on it. Crito just lets it go, and goes back to the earlier issue of the consequences for Socrates' friends. Is Socrates thinking that his friends will be in danger of reprisals if he escapes? Yes, it seems that he is (and he returns to emphasize the risk to them at 53a/b). This of course quite neutralizes

Crito's argument: <u>no point in appealing to the bad effects on your friends</u> <u>if you *don't* do something, when the effects on them if you *do* are likely</u> <u>to be at least as bad.</u>

Crito, understandably quite wound up, now makes a longer speech (45a–46a) in which he fires off all his remaining ammunition in an emotional and haphazard sort of way. Socrates shouldn't think of the risk to his friends, or the expense—anyway, the expense won't be all that great. Nor should he bother about the fact that escape into exile would mean going back on things he said at his trial. (We shall soon see, at 46b–46d and 52c, that this cuts no ice whatever with Socrates, for whom being consistent, true to himself and his reasons for acting, is a very important value.)

Next, Crito goes on, Socrates is acting wrongly in giving up his life when he could save it, and so falling in with his enemies' wishes. Crito doesn't tell us whether he thinks that for Socrates to give up his life when he could save it would be wrong *just because* it means success for his enemies, or whether it is an intrinsically wrong thing to do—as some have thought suicide intrinsically wrong—or for some other reason again. Which of these he has in mind actually makes quite a difference to what he is saying, but he is in no state for precise thinking. Now seriously overheating, he first accuses Socrates of showing no concern for his children, then of showing a lack of courage (45d). (Considering the courage required for what Socrates actually does intend to do, the latter charge seems particularly absurd—the one about his children Socrates will deal with later.) Running out of steam, Crito now returns to his complaint about the damage to Socrates' friends' reputations, begs Socrates to agree with him, and comes to a stop.

In his distress and anxiety Crito has become pretty offensive in his last couple of paragraphs. But this Socrates overlooks, with a kind remark about Crito's warm feelings, and takes control of the dialogue. The thinking immediately becomes slower and calmer, and better organized. He returns to the first point Crito made—the one about reputation—and asks whose opinion we should respect, those of the wise or the foolish, those of the many or those of the expert? Crito trots along giving the obvious answers, the way his discussion partners usually do when Socrates gets into gear. So in this case we shouldn't be listening to the majority, but to someone who understands what it is to be just, to act rightly, to live well or as one should. Otherwise we shall damage our souls, as we would have damaged our bodies by listening to the majority rather than the doctor in a matter of physical health. The crucial question is whether it is right for Socrates to try to escape—all this stuff about money, reputations, and bringing up children is of no real consequence (48c).

Let's just pause for a moment. One thing we should not do is read philosophy uncritically. Isn't there a whiff of moral fanaticism about what Socrates is now saying? What damage to his soul exactly? And why should it be so frightful? And if his friends' reputations and his children's upbringing are on the line, mightn't he be prepared to risk a little damage to his soul? After all, he wouldn't think much of anyone who wasn't prepared to risk physical injury for the sake of friends and family. Admittedly, we have been told (back at 47e–48a) that the soul, or more accurately "that part of us, whatever it is, which is concerned with justice and injustice," is much more valuable than the body. But we haven't been told why or how; and there has been no explanation of why it should be *so* valuable that the prospect of damage to it instantly overrides any little matters like friends' reputations or the well-being of one's children. And besides, if children are not well cared for, might that not damage "that part of *them*, whatever it is, which is concerned with justice and injustice"? It looks as if Socrates needed a different discussion partner, someone who might have started calling for answers to a few of these questions.

But let us hear Socrates out, and get a view of the full picture, as he argues that it would be wrong for him to escape into exile. First he asks Crito to agree that doing someone a wrong is always wrong, even when done in response to a wrong done to you (49a–49e). Revenge may be sweet, but it is not permissible. The strategic importance of this is easy to see: if it is accepted, then whether anyone has wronged Socrates—the state, the jurors, his accusers—becomes irrelevant; the only question is whether he himself would be doing a wrong in following Crito's plan. Clearly Socrates does not expect there to be widespread agreement on this point. He knows only too well that there are many who hold that retaliation is permissible, even that it is positively right. But it is Crito he is trying to convince, and the two of

It is essential that we read philosophy critically, so that Socrates' claim that the soul is more valuable than the body should not pass unchallenged; Socrates has not explained why this is so, particularly when salvation of the soul—by doing what is right and in that way serving justice—overrides the reputations of one's friends and the happy upbringing of one's children. This photograph of a section of a fresco painting by Giovan Francesco Penni showing Justice, seated, holding scales in her left hand and her right hand on the neck of an ostrich, is in the Raphael Room, in Rome, Italy.

them have evidently been here in discussion before—"our former opinion" he calls it. And Crito agrees: "I stand by it."

Socrates now puts forward two much less controversial premises: <u>doing harm to people is wrong</u> (49c), and <u>breaking a fair agreement is wrong</u> (49e). He is now about to argue that if he tries to escape he will be doing both. The injured parties would be the state of Athens and its laws; he imagines them coming forward, personified, to put their case.

In the first place, he would be doing them harm (50a–50b), indeed he would be "intending their destruction." That sounds odd—surely the only thing Socrates would be intending is to escape execution? But the next sentence tells us what is meant: if what he proposes to do were taken as an example, the result would be the collapse of the law and hence also of

Integrity: it was of the utmost importance to Socrates that his subsequent behavior should be consistent with all that he had said in his own defense. Socrates is shown addressing the Athenian court in this 1750 engraving by L. P. Boitard, while the figure of Justice stands behind him.

the state, neither of which can survive if private individuals ignore the decisions of the courts. What we have here is an appeal to a very familiar moral argument: "What would happen if everybody behaved like that?" When I do something, it is as if I were giving everyone else my permission to do the same, and I have to consider the consequences of *that*, not just of my individual action. The German Immanuel Kant (1724–1804), some would say the most influential philosopher of modern times, made this the basic principle of morality (though he found a rather more complicated way of stating it). We have all heard of it, we have all had it thrown at us, and here it is popping up in 400 BCE.

In the second place, they suggest (50c), Socrates would be breaking an agreement. But from here to 51d what the laws and the state have to say does not seem to be about an *agreement* at all, in any normal sense—no voluntary consent to anything on the part of Socrates is in question. It might be better described as being about obligations of gratitude, or about the deference

owed by a creature to its creator, or both. The burden of this paragraph is that the Athenian state, which is compared to a parent, made Socrates what he is; and he is not dissatisfied with how it did it. So he is bound by its wishes, and it is ridiculous to suppose that he might have a right of retaliation against it.

Eighteenth-century German philosopher Immanuel Kant articulated the same moral principle as Socrates, though in a more complex form, that when one does something, it is as if one is giving everyone else permission to do the same.

The last point really ought to be unnecessary, since Socrates has already said that retaliation is wrong anyway. But he can be seen as covering himself twice: even if retaliation were sometimes right, as many think it is, it would still not be right in this case, where the parentlike state is the other party. As to his being bound by the state's wishes, this totalitarian conception of the state's powers and the corresponding view of parental authority is more stipulated than justified in this passage. That isn't surprising, because it wouldn't be at all easy to justify the doctrine that the state, by virtue of its role in the lives of human individuals, thereby acquires the right to dispose of them much as if they were inanimate artifacts made for its own purposes. A state may do a lot for its citizens, but can it conceivably do so much that they can lay claim to no purposes of their own beyond those it allows them? And once we grant that Socrates might be allowed some purposes of his own independent of

Political authority has absolute control

Socrates lived voluntarily in Athens all his life, clearly indicating his consent to the authority of the city's institutions. This view of the ancient city is a detail from an 1851 engraving by Henry Winkles.

the will of Athens, then might not staying alive (if that is what he wants) be one of them? Crito, were he not the perfect yes-man, could have had rather more to say at this stage.

However, at 51d Socrates' imaginary antagonists introduce a point which, if correct, makes a very big difference: Socrates has of his own free will entered into an agreement with them to respect and obey the laws. Not that he ever signed a document or made an official statement; but his behavior was a sufficient indication of his agreement. For the law allowed him, once an adult, to take his possessions and leave Athens without any material penalty. He stayed. Nor has he ever in his seventy years been away even temporarily, except on military service. At his trial he made it clear that he had no interest in exile as a possible alternative sentence. Taken together, this is clear voluntary consent to the institutions of Athens. Does he now (contrary to what he avowed at 49e) intend to break his agreement?

Much of Socrates' argument has been conducted at a high level of principle, sometimes dizzily high—as when he said that compared with the importance of doing what is right, matters of reputation (his friends' as well as his own) and the upbringing of children were of no account. But here in the closing pages of *Crito*, between 52c and the end, there are signs of him covering his back. Whether he wants to be sure of convincing those not convinced of his lofty principles, or whether he isn't himself altogether happy to let the entire issue rest on them, the fact is that reputations, the risks to his friends, his prospects in exile, and the education of his children now make a reappearance.

Not many pages back Socrates was telling Crito not to bother about the opinion of the crowd. But "the laws and the state" think it is at least worth mentioning that he is in danger of making himself a laughingstock (53a), and of hearing many deprecatory things about himself (53e), and of giving the jurors reason to think that they made the right decision (53b/c). (More important to one holding Socrates' principles is that he himself would be ashamed if he were to go back on what he so proudly said at his trial [52c]—his own integrity ought to mean more to him than that.) He should think of the practical consequences: if he escapes his friends will be in danger (53b); his life in exile will be unrewarding and demeaning (53b–53e). And finally (54a), what will it benefit his children? Is he to bring them up in Thessaly (Thessaly of all places!), exiles themselves? And if they are to grow up in Athens, what difference to them whether he is dead or merely absent? His friends will see to their education in either case.

The laws have one last card to play, well-known and much used by moralists from earliest times right down to our own: the old fire-and-brimstone maneuver. Should Socrates offend against them, they say, he

[margin annotation, handwritten: disapproval]

L. P. Boitard's 1750 engraving shows Socrates holding the cup of hemlock that he would eventually drink to enforce the Athenian court's death sentence.

can expect an uncomfortable reception in the afterlife. The laws of the underworld are their brothers, and will avenge them.

Finally, Socrates speaks again in his own person (54d). His closing words broach another perennial topic: the relationship between morals and religion. Some have held (and many have disagreed with them) that morality is impossible without belief in a god. There is no reason to attribute that view to Socrates. But he does appear to be doing something just as time-honored as the fire-and-brimstone trick, and a good deal more comforting: claiming divine moral inspiration. "These things I seem to hear, Crito . . . and these words re-echo within me, so that I can hear no others. . . . Let us then act in this way, since this is the way the god is leading."

Neoclassical Venetian sculptor Antonio Canova created this late-eighteenth-century relief of Crito closing the eyes of the dead Socrates.

The dialogue is over; I hope you have enjoyed reading it. Moral problems are notoriously hard to settle, not just when several people are trying to reach agreement, but even when they are trying to make up their own minds as individuals. We have seen a little of why this should be: so many factors, of so many different types, are involved. Should you do A or not? Well, what will the consequences be if you do? There may be consequences for your friends, your family, and others, as well as those for you yourself. And what if you don't? How do the consequences compare? Alternatively, never mind the consequences for a moment; just ask whether you can do A consistently with your own view of yourself— would it involve betraying ideals that till then you had valued and tried to live up to? How will you *feel* about having done it? Or again, however pleasant the consequences may be, would it run contrary to some duty, or some obligations you have incurred? Obligations to whom?—and might you not be in breach of other obligations if you *don't* do it? Do obligations to friends and family take precedence over duties toward the state, or vice versa? And if you have a religion what does *it* say about the choice?

All this complexity is only latent in *Crito*, because Socrates manages to make all the relevant factors come out either neutral (it won't make much difference to his children either way, nor to his friends) or all pointing in the same direction. But it doesn't take much imagination to see the potential for agonizing moral dilemmas.

Some people expect philosophy to tell us the answers to moral problems. But unless it can somehow impose simplicity on the complexities we have been looking at, the prospects for that don't look good. For it would have to show us, convincingly, that there was just *one* right way to balance out all the various considerations. Socrates was going for simplification when (starting at 48c) he tried to make the whole thing turn on just one issue. Kant, whom I mentioned earlier, went for simplification in basing morality on a single principle closely related to the familiar "what would happen if everyone did that?" Some try to simplify in another way, advising us not to think in terms of duties and obligations but only of the consequences of our own proposed actions for everyone whom they will affect. We shall see more of this kind of view in Chapter 5.

His
tory
and

Phi
lofo
phy

DAVID HUME

Efq.

THREE

How Do We Know?
Hume's *Of Miracles*

●

MANY—INCLUDING YOUR PRESENT GUIDE—regard the Scotsman David Hume (1711–76) as the greatest of all philosophers who have written in English. He was of wide-ranging intellect: his multivolume *History of England* had the effect that in his lifetime he was equally well-known as a historian, and he also wrote essays on political (mainly constitutional) questions and on economics. All of this he saw as contributing to a single broad project, the study of human nature. His youthful masterpiece, published in 1739–40, is called *A Treatise of Human Nature*; in three books it deals with human beliefs, emotions, and moral judgments. What are they, and what produces them?

David Hume is recognized as one of the greatest philosophers to have written in the English language. The eighteenth-century Scottish philosopher, economist, and historian is shown here in an image from around 1766.

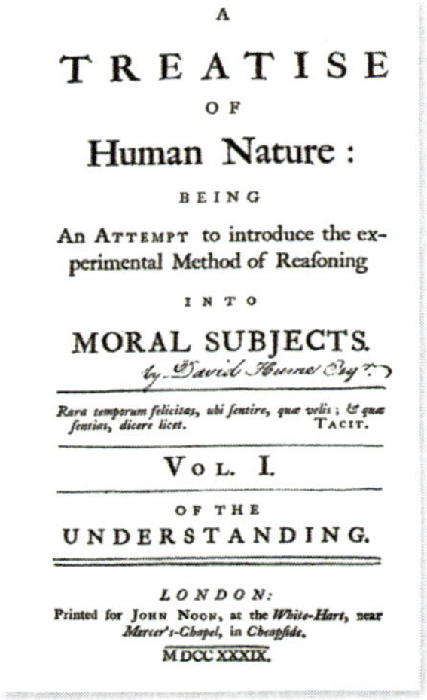

A

TREATISE

OF

Human Nature :

BEING

An ATTEMPT to introduce the experimental Method of Reasoning

INTO

MORAL SUBJECTS.

by David Hume Esq?

Rara temporum felicitas, ubi sentire, quæ velis ; & quæ sentias, dicere licet. TACIT.

VOL. I.

OF THE

UNDERSTANDING.

LONDON:
Printed for JOHN NOON, at the *White-Hart*, near *Mercer's-Chapel*, in *Cheapside.*
M DCC XXXIX.

A Treatise of Human Nature, which deals with human beliefs, emotions, and moral judgments, was published when Hume was only twenty-eight years old. The title page of the first edition (1739–40) of the philosopher's masterpiece is shown here.

Hume's writings on these questions are shaped by a deeply held conviction about what human beings are. Equally important to him was a conviction about what we aren't, a particular delusion which had to be overcome before anything more positive would have a chance of taking hold of our minds. Remember that most great philosophy doesn't just add/subtract one or two facts to/from our previous beliefs; it removes a whole way of thinking and replaces it with another. There may be a lot of minute detail within it, but just stand back a bit and you will see that it is large-scale stuff.

The conception that Hume wanted to root out had its basis in religious belief. Taking very seriously the saying that God created us in his own image, it saw us as hybrid beings, in this world but not entirely of it. Part of us, our bodies, are natural objects, subject to natural laws and processes; but we also have immortal souls, endowed with reason and an understanding of morality—this is what makes us images of God. Animals are quite different. They have no souls,

Hume was no supporter of the doctrine that humans are created in the image of God; he held that on the contrary we are highly developed animals, parts of the natural world. Shown here is God creating Eve in his image, one in a series of early-sixteenth-century stained-glass windows depicting the book of Genesis at the Church of the Madeleine, in Troyes, France.

but are just very subtle and complex machines, nothing more. The really significant line comes between us and them, not between us and God. Hume wanted to move it: we are not inferior little gods but somewhat superior middle-sized animals.

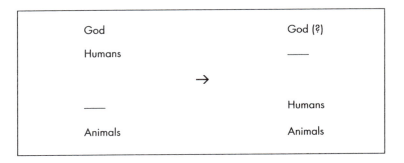

God	God (?)
Humans	———
→	
———	Humans
Animals	Animals

Don't miss the added "?," top right. The left-hand column invites us to overestimate human reason. Once we get it in proper perspective we shall see both that we have drawn the line in the wrong place, and that our attempts even to think about what might be above the line are doomed to failure: we just aren't up to it.

Hume therefore has a great deal to say about the role of reason in our lives; he argues that it isn't nearly as big, or of the same kind, as his opponents thought. It then follows that much of what they took human reason to do must in fact be done by something else: the mechanics of human nature, about which he developed an extensive theory, a piece of early cognitive science as we would call it nowadays. But when Hume writes directly about religious belief (as he does quite a lot; see the bibliography), he leaves the grand theory on the shelf and applies common sense and everyday human observation. So in his essay

Of Miracles we have another classic piece of philosophical writing that starts on your doorstep, if not actually in your living room.

However, we mustn't assume that everything here is completely familiar. Hume is going to argue that if we believe that a miracle has occurred, when our evidence consists in other people's reports (as it virtually always does), then we hold this belief contrary to reason, since our reasons for believing that the alleged miracle did *not* occur must be at least as strong as our reasons for supposing that it did; in fact, he thinks, they are always stronger. This was a topic that he needed to approach carefully, for two reasons. Not twenty years before he published *Of Miracles* one Thomas Woolston had spent the last few years of his life in prison for saying that the biblical reports of Christ's resurrection were not adequate evidence for belief in so unlikely an event; what Hume was now about to say was by no means unrelated. Second, Hume really wanted to change the way his contemporaries, especially his compatriots, thought about religion. He couldn't do that if they didn't read him, so he had to lead them in gently.

Hence the "Tillotson connection" that Hume parades in the opening paragraph. What could be better than to be able to say that your views are just a development of an argument recently proposed by an archbishop? Except perhaps, to be able to add that the archbishop's argument was a decisive refutation of a specifically Roman Catholic doctrine? Hume's public, most of them in varying degrees hostile to Catholicism, would feel a comfortable warm glow . . . and read on.

Before we look at the argument itself, one more question: why does Hume find it important to write about the evidence for miracles? It is part of his plan for a systematic treatment of the grounds of religious belief, and it was customary to think of these as being of two kinds. On the one hand there were those which human beings, going on their own experience and

John Tillotson, shown here in an etching from 1740, was archbishop of Canterbury from 1691 until his death in 1694. His *Discourse Against Transubstantiation* was published in 1684, about sixty years before Hume published *Of Miracles*.

using their own reason, could work out for themselves. On the other, there were those that came from revelation, that is to say from a sacred text or some other authority. But these present a further problem, because you could have fraudulent texts and bogus authorities; so how to tell the genuine ones? The answer was that genuine revelations are connected with the occurrence of miracles: hence their importance, as certificates of religious authority. (Ultimately, they are issued by the highest possible authority; the widely accepted view, which Hume here takes over, had it that miracles were violations of laws of nature, and therefore could only be performed by God or those God had entrusted with divine powers.) That we can never have good reason to believe in a miracle was therefore a pretty subversive claim; it amounted to saying that human reason cannot tell the bona fide revelation from the bogus.

genuine/real

So now to Hume's argument. It starts at a point we all know well, because we all frequently rely on things that other people have told us. Mostly there has been no problem, but occasionally what we were told turned out to be false. Occasionally we have heard contradictory things from two people, so we knew that at least one of them was wrong even if we never found out which. And we also know a little about what leads to false reports: self-interest, protection of others, defense of a cause dear to one's heart, the wish to have a good story to tell, simple sincere mistake, uncritical belief of earlier reports, mischief, and so on. Most of us have sometime in our lives gone wrong in most of these ways ourselves, so that it isn't just from observation of others (as some of Hume's words might be taken to suggest) that we acquire this knowledge. We all know that human testimony is sometimes to be treated with caution, and under certain circumstances with a great deal of caution.

Suppose I were to tell you that last week I drove, on a normal weekday morning just before midday, right across London from north to south, and didn't see a single person or vehicle on the way—not a car, not a bicycle, not a pedestrian; everyone just happened to be somewhere else as I was passing. You might wonder whether it was an absurdly exaggerated way of saying that the roads were unusually quiet, or whether I was testing your gullibility, or recounting a dream, or maybe going mad, but one option you would not seriously entertain is that what I had said was true. Almost anything, you would tell yourself, however unlikely, is more likely than that.

That would be very reasonable of you. Even if what I said was in fact true (which is just about conceivable, since nobody was under any compulsion to be on my route at that time, so they *might* all have decided to be somewhere else), it still wouldn't be at all reasonable of you to believe it, if your only reason for believing it was that I had said so. Had you been with me and seen the empty streets yourself things might be different; but we are talking about the case in which you are reliant on my testimony.

Perhaps you can see the shape of Hume's argument beginning to appear. Given what its role is to be in underpinning religious belief, a miraculous event must surely be one which our experience tells us is highly improbable. For if it were the sort of thing that can quite easily happen, then any old charlatan with a bit of luck or good timing could seize the opportunity to qualify as having divine authority. But if it

fraud

is highly improbable, only the most reliable testimony will be strong enough to establish it. Forced to choose between two improbabilities, the wise, who as Hume tells us proportion belief to evidence, will opt for the alternative they find less improbable. So this will have to be the testimony of such witnesses, that its falsehood would be more improbable than the occurrence of the events it relates. And that is a tall order, since, as we have seen, the events must be very improbable indeed.

Now this leaves it perfectly possible that we might, *in theory*, have testimonial evidence that was strong enough. But it is enough to create serious doubt whether we do, *in fact*, have adequate evidence for any miracle. We know that eyewitnesses can be mistaken, or intentionally deceived. Many of us have had the experience of finding ourselves in disagreement with someone else who was also an eyewitness to the events reported, often within a day or two of the events themselves. Many reports of the miraculous come to us from people who were not eyewitnesses, and were writing or speaking years after the events in question. Most such reports come from adherents of the religion which these alleged miracles are used to support. A court of law would take the possibility that witnesses of this kind were unreliable very seriously indeed—in some cases so seriously that it wouldn't even be prepared to hear them testify.

Are there any reports of miracles which escape such doubts? It sounds as if we might have to trawl through the whole of recorded history to answer that question. But that, Hume thinks, won't be necessary. For it isn't

Hume, like many of his contemporaries, thought that an event could only be a miracle if it contravened the laws of nature. But then, he argued, our reasons for believing a report of a miraculous event could never be stronger than our reasons for disbelieving it. The miracle of the loaves and fishes, in which Jesus is reported to have multiplied just a few loaves of bread and a few fish to feed thousands, is depicted in this manuscript illumination from the fifteenth-century book of hours *Les très riches heures du duc de Berry*.

Etauit ūenila gaudetē aim letiaa quī
lem et connie tristiaa fuistis ut enultetis
tam facite et faciemini ab uberibus
omnes qui diligitis eam consolacionis uir. ps.

just that a miracle has to be extremely improbable. It has to be in a sense *impossible*—contrary to a law of nature ("instead of being only marvellous, . . . really miraculous"). That was Hume's definition, and the one he expected his audience to accept. And this enables us to state the argument again in a slightly different, and more decisive, form—the form Hume preferred.

We receive a report of something—for convenience call it The Event—supposed to be miraculous. So we are asked to believe that The Event occurred, and that this was contrary to a law of nature. For us to have good reason to believe that an event of that kind would have been contrary to a law of nature, it must be contrary to all our experience, and to our best theories of how nature works. But if that is so then we must have very strong reason to believe that The Event did *not* occur—in fact the strongest reason we ever do have for believing anything of that sort.

So what reason do we have on the other side—to believe that it *did* occur? Answer: the report—in other words, the fact that it is *said* to have occurred. Could that possibly be so strong as to overpower the contrary reasons and win the day for The Event? No, says Hume, it could (in theory) be of equal strength, but never of greater. There might be such a thing as testimony, given by sufficiently well-placed witnesses, of the right sort of character, under the right sort of circumstances, that as a matter of natural (psychological) law it was bound to be true. But that would only mean that we had our strongest kind of evidence both for The Event and against it, and the rational response would be not belief but bewilderment and indecision.

Note the parenthetical words *in theory*. Hume doesn't think that we ever find this situation in practice, and gives a number of reasons why not. Had he lived in our time he might have added that psychological research has uncovered a number of surprising facts about the *unreliability* of human memory and testimony, but shows no sign of homing in on any set of conditions under which their reliability is completely assured. Nor should we expect it to, given the range of disruptive factors which Hume lists.

This, in essence, was Hume's argument. Unsurprisingly, it has provoked much discussion, and still does. Here are a couple of points, to give the flavor. They also nicely illustrate two features frequent in philosophical discussion and indeed in debate generally, so well worth being on the lookout for: there is the criticism which, while perfectly true in itself, misses the point; and there is the objection that an argument "proves too much."

Hume, it may be said, based his argument on the thought that a miracle must be (at least) extremely improbable. But won't his opponents just deny that? They, after all, are believers. So whereas they might regard a report that—to take Hume's own example—Queen Elizabeth I rose from the dead as far beneath serious consideration, just as Hume himself would, they may regard the alleged miracle of Christ's resurrection as not very improbable at all, given who they take Christ to have been. Hasn't Hume just begged the question against them—not so much proved that they are wrong as simply assumed it?

Painting of the resurrection on the organ loft of the parish church of St. Gebhard, in Maierhöfen, Allgau, Germany.

But we should reply on his behalf that this mistakes what Hume was doing. He was asking what reasons there may be for forming religious beliefs in the first place. That the world may look very different, and different arguments appear reasonable, when one has already formed them, he would not for one moment dispute. Nor need he dispute it: it has no bearing on the central issue, which is whether a miracle can be proved, "so as to be the foundation of a system of religion."

So that objection is simply off target. The second is not, and gives Hume more trouble. Doesn't his argument show that it could never be reasonable for us to revise our views about the laws of nature? But that is the main way in which science makes progress; so if *that* is irrational, then any charge that belief in miracles is irrational begins to look rather less serious. "If I'm no worse than Newton and Einstein and company," the believer will say, "I'm not too bothered."

Why might it be thought that Hume's argument has gone over the top in this way? Well, suppose we have very good reason to think that something is a law of nature: all our experience to date fits in with it, and our best current scientific theory supports it. Now suppose that some scientists report an experimental result which conflicts with it. Doesn't Hume's argument tell us that we ought just to dismiss their report on the spot? Our evidence that what they report to have happened cannot happen is as good as any evidence we ever have; on the other side of the question we have just—their testimony. Isn't that exactly the situation he was talking about in regard to reports of miracles?

Hume appears to be trying to preempt some such criticism when he writes, "For I own that otherwise [i.e., when it is not a question of being the foundation of a system of religion] there may possibly be miracles, or violations of the usual course of nature, of such a kind as to admit of proof from human testimony. . . ." And he goes on to describe an imaginary case (philosophers often use imaginary cases to test the force of an argument) in which there are found in all human societies reports of an eight-day darkness, which agree with each other exactly as to when the darkness began and when it lifted. Then, he says, it is clear that we ought to accept the report, and start

One of the main sources of advance in the natural sciences is the discovery of facts in conflict with what have up to then been thought to be laws of nature. It may appear that Hume's argument about belief in miracles has the consequence that it could never be rational to believe in such facts. But does it really? Hume's argument about the possibility that miracles occur appears to suggest that it could never be reasonable for us to revise our ideas about the laws of nature. Since this is the way in which scientists such as Newton and Einstein advanced our knowledge of the scientific world, however, calling it irrational makes any charge that belief in miracles is irrational seem less serious. German-born theoretical physicist Albert Einstein developed his theory of general relativity over the years 1907–15. To test the theory, scientists and engineers constructed a near-perfect gyroscope, in which the Nobel Prize–winning scientist's image is refracted here.

considering what the cause of this extraordinary event might have been. But he does not tell us precisely what it is about this example that makes the difference. And that was what we needed to know.

I think Hume could have made a better, and certainly a clearer, response to the threat. He might have said that in circumstances such as I have just outlined (last paragraph but one) the scientific community probably would *not* believe the report, and that they would be perfectly rational not to, until several of them had *repeated the experiment* and got exactly the same result. Belief in it would then no longer be a matter of testimony alone, but also of widespread observation. We can, and do, demand that scientific results be replicable; we can't demand a rerun of a miracle. Where for any reason no rerun is possible, those making the improbable assertion have it too easy, and we ought to be as cautious in science as we should be in matters religious.

It may be, though we cannot be certain, that this is what Hume was trying to say. In the imaginary situation he describes, the report of the eight-day darkness is found in *all* cultures. At a time when communication was slow and cumbersome, and likely to be partial and inaccurate, perhaps he took his story to be one in which it was beyond doubt that all these different peoples had *independently* made precisely the same observations, so that the situation was the equivalent of running an experiment several times with exactly the same result. As I say, we cannot be certain—not even Hume, one of the best philosophical writers in this respect, is clear all the time. But we can be fairly certain that that was not *all* he was trying to say. For at the end of the paragraph from which the quotation above is taken, we find this: "The decay, corruption, and dissolution of nature, is an event rendered probable by so many analogies, that any phenomenon, which seems to have a tendency towards that catastrophe, comes within the reach of human testimony, if that testimony be very extensive and uniform."

Or in other words, the alleged eight-day darkness would indeed be very unusual, but there is nothing especially unusual about nature behaving out of the normal pattern from time to time. So we have no reason to regard such a thing as *impossible*, and therefore there is no real comparison with the case of a miracle at all. We could spend a long time among the details of Hume's essay *Of Miracles*. Many have. But our tour must move on.

FOUR

What Am I?
An Unknown Buddhist on the Self:
King Milinda's Chariot

•

IT IS GENERALLY TRUE OF INDIAN PHILOSOPHY that we do not know much about the people who wrote it. If we know their names, the region in which they lived, and their dates within fifty years, that counts as scholarly success. But in the case of the *Milindapañha*, the *Questions of King Milinda*, no such "success" has been achieved—we really know next to nothing. Here a Buddhist monk, Nagasena, debates with a regional king and answers his questions. Nagasena is probably a real figure, grown legendary; King Milinda is generally thought to be Menander, one of the Greek rulers in northwest India left over from the conquests of Alexander

This detail of the relief on the North Torana of the Great Stupa at Sanchi (dating from sometime between the first century BCE and the first century CE), in Bhopal, India, depicts events from the life of Buddha, including processions and battles.

King Milinda may be Menander I, an Indo-Greek king who lived from 165 or 155 BCE until 130 BCE. King Menander is shown here on the face of a coin from Punjab.

the Great. Even that is speculative—so let us just go straight to the text.

Only a few lines into it a shock awaits us. Plato's *Crito*, we saw, is built of elements nearly all of which most readers will have found quite familiar. Hume's argument in *Of Miracles* aimed to start from everyday commonsense observations about testimony plus an unsurprising definition of a miracle, and then arrive at a remarkable conclusion by showing that it is an inevitable consequence. But sometimes authors will adopt different tactics, pitching us straight in at the deep end with an assertion which seems frankly preposterous. We should learn to ride out the shock and read on, seeking to discover what the preposterous assertion really amounts to (it may be what it seems, or it may just be an unusual way of saying something rather less startling), and why they made it. Notice that "why they made it" means two things, both important: their reasons for thinking it true—and their motives for being interested in it, what they are aiming at. All of these points are highly relevant to the passage we are about to look at.

First, the shock. The party gathers; the king asks Nagasena's name, Nagasena tells him: "Sire, I am known as Nagasena"—but then adds that this word "Nagasena" is only "a mere name, because there is no person as such that is found." What can he possibly mean? One would have thought that Nagasena was a person, and he has just told Milinda his name; but immediately it turns out that the name is not the name of a person. So Nagasena isn't a person after all, and this even though *he* has just told the king how *he* is known and how *his* fellow monks address *him*. What is going on here?

The king, who is evidently experienced in this kind of discussion (and also has considerable prior knowledge of Buddhism), doesn't despair but sets out to get to the bottom of it. Realizing that Nagasena wasn't just speaking of himself, but intended the point he was making (whatever it may have been) to apply equally to everyone, he starts drawing what he takes to be absurd consequences from the monk's view. If it is true, then nobody ever does anything, right or wrong, nobody ever achieves anything, suffers anything. There is no such thing as a murder, for there is no person who dies. And then a little joke about Nagasena's status: there was no one who taught him, and no one who ordained him. The tactic is common in debates of all kinds: here are a number of things which we all unhesitatingly take to be true; is Nagasena really saying that they are all false? Or is he going to tell us that his view, if properly understood, doesn't have that consequence? Nagasena never takes that challenge up directly. By the end of the chapter he has given a hint, from which we can reconstruct what he might have said had he done so. But for the moment the king continues, falling into question-and-answer style reminiscent of many of Plato's dialogues.

Milinda's questioning in this passage is structured by the Buddhist doctrine of the "five aggregates," according to which what we call a human being is a complex of five elements. Milinda calls them material form, feeling (by which they seem to have understood pleasure, pain, and indifference), perception, mental formations (i.e., our dispositions, our character), and consciousness. Exactly what these are we need not bother about, so long as we have some rough idea: the point is that *the person* is not to be identified with any of them.

That is probably what most of us would say, on a little reflection. Are we our feelings? No, we are what has the feelings, not the feelings themselves. Are we our perceptions? No, for the same reason. Are we our dispositions, our character? Well again, no—because dispositions, characters are tendencies to behave in certain ways; and we aren't the tendencies but rather *what has* those tendencies. Likewise, we aren't the consciousness; we are *whatever it is* that is conscious. The fifth item (the one that Milinda actually put first) might be more contentious, however. Mightn't the material element, that is, the body, be the thing that is conscious, has the dispositions, the perceptions, the feelings? When asked, in effect, whether the body is Nagasena, why is Nagasena so quick to say that it isn't?

When someone presents a point as if it were pretty obvious when it doesn't seem obvious to you at all, it is good tactics to look for something unspoken lying behind it. Perhaps they are assuming that a self, a person, must be something rather pure and lofty—notice the studiously repulsive description of the body with which the king prefaces his question. Or that a self must be a permanent, unchanging thing, quite unlike a body, perhaps even capable of surviving death. Either of those assumptions might have come from earlier philosophical/religious conceptions—back to that in a moment. Or maybe from some such thought as this: matter doesn't move itself (just leave a lump of it lying around and see how much it moves), whereas an animal does—so there must be something nonmaterial in it moving its matter. Or: even if matter does move it doesn't make coherent, directed, intelligent movements—so a body needs something to direct it.

These thoughts were commonplace long before *Questions of King Milinda* was written. Remember the importance Socrates attaches to the well-being of his soul in *Crito*; or go on to read Plato's *Phaedo*—the follow-up to *Crito*, about Socrates' very last discussion and death. "Hold it a moment," you will say, "that's Greece, whereas this is India." True, but very similar ideas are found (even earlier) in the Brahminical writings sacred to Hinduism. Admittedly, Buddhism quite consciously broke away from the Brahminical tradition. But the main points of contention were animal sacrifice and the caste system (which Buddhism abandoned along with all extreme forms of asceticism), so that a great deal of that

Brahminical writings sacred to Hinduism also contain thoughts regarding the questions discussed in *Questions of King Milinda*, and although Buddhism broke away from Brahminical tradition, the points of contention were limited to the caste system and animal sacrifice. This hand-colored French lithograph of a brahmin presenting an outcaste with alms is by Marlet et Companie after an original drawing by Geringer.

tradition remained and formed the background to Buddhism as well. The idea of cyclical rebirth to further lives of suffering, and the hope of escape from the cycle into a state of liberation (the Buddhist *nirvana* and the Hindu *moksha*), are equally part of both.

Knowing these things may help us a little in understanding the prompt "No, sire" with which Nagasena answers this sequence of questions. But it doesn't help as much as we might wish, because it gives no hint as to why he should make the same response to the king's last question, whether then Nagasena is something else, something different from the five "aggregates." If anything, it might lead us to expect that he would say that yes, it was something different, something that could leave the body and later inhabit another, that could be having certain feelings and perceptions now, and could have quite different ones in the future. But again he says, "No, sire"—it is *not* something else. So the puzzle remains. And Milinda's next remark is puzzling too: he accuses the monk of having spoken a falsehood, for apparently "there is no Nagasena." But Nagasena never said there was—quite the contrary, it was his perplexing remark that there *wasn't* a person "Nagasena" which set the discussion going.

You do meet traffic jams like this sometimes, and it would be a poor guide who tried to cover it up. We need some creative reading at this stage. For instance: are we to think of the king as just getting confused, and losing track of what has been said? Or is it that he simply can't believe that there is no such person, and therefore thought that Nagasena was bound to answer yes to at least one of his questions; since he answered no to all of them, at least one answer must have been false, and that is the falsehood the king means when he says "You, revered sir, . . . have spoken a falsehood"? Of those two (perhaps you can think of another?), I prefer the second. It fits better with the feeling one gets from the chapter as a whole that the king is supposed to have a mistaken view of the nature of the self about which Nagasena puts him right.

He does so (after briefly teasing Milinda about his pampered lifestyle) by asking a parallel series of questions about the king's chariot. This tradition makes constant use of similes, parallels, and analogies; listeners are brought to feel comfortable with something they find problematic by

The monk Nagasena asks the king a series of questions about his chariot to help explain his view about the relationship between a whole and its parts. This tondo of a red-figure Attic cup (ca. 460 or 470 BCE) showing the warrior Triptolemus with the goddess Korē was created by the so-called Aberdeen Painter.

coming to see it as similar to, or of the same kind as, something else with which they are already familiar. Here the hope is that once the king has answered no to all the questions about the chariot, he will see how Nagasena could return the same answer to all his questions about the person.

And he does come to see it, by the end of the chapter. But first let me mention something which no study of this text by itself could reveal, but which would surely have had an effect on anyone of Milinda's obvious learning and intelligence. In using a chariot as a parallel to a person, Nagasena is doing something both strongly reminiscent of, and at the same time shockingly at odds with, a metaphor well-known within their common philosophical culture.

Plato famously compared the self to a chariot. A good deal earlier, in the Indian tradition, the *Katha Upanishad* does the same (see the bibliography). Is it now Nagasena's turn? Well, not exactly. It is as if the author were alluding to the tradition precisely to highlight his rejection of it. In Plato we read of a charioteer trying to control one obedient horse (reason) and one disobedient horse (the appetites); the *Katha Upanishad* compares the self to someone riding in a chariot, the intellect to the charioteer directing the senses, which are the horses. Nagasena doesn't mention any horses. More importantly, he doesn't mention a charioteer, let alone a rider distinct from the charioteer. That is the very picture he is reacting against. There is no permanent presence, the self, directing or overseeing. This author, in using the hallowed simile of the chariot but using it differently, is simultaneously putting his own view and signaling, to his cultural circle, just what he is rejecting.

So now the monk, following exactly the same pattern, questions the king: "Is the axle the chariot?—are the wheels the chariot? . . ." Milinda repeatedly answers no. That isn't surprising—but much as Nagasena's answers to his questions were fairly unsurprising except for the last, so *one* of Milinda's answers will raise nearly every reader's eyebrows. This time, however, it isn't the last but the next to last. Nagasena asks whether then the chariot is "the pole, the axle, the wheels, . . . the reins and the goad all together." Most of us would say "Yes; so long as we are not talking about these parts lying around in a heap but rather *in the proper arrangement*, that's exactly what a chariot is." But Milinda just says, "No, revered sir."

We shall shortly find out what lies behind this rather odd response. For the moment let us just notice that the king, having answered no to all the questions, has put himself in the same position as had Nagasena, who immediately throws Milinda's own earlier words back at him: "Where then is the chariot you say you came in? You, sire, have spoken a falsehood . . ."—and gets a round of applause even

Nagasena asks King Milinda whether the parts of the chariot—the pole, the axle, the wheels—together are the chariot, but the king answers no, *chariot* exists as a mere designation. This Etruscan chariot wheel, from about 530 BCE, was found in Monteleone di Spoleto (the ancient Roman city of Brufa) in the province of Perugia, Italy.

from Milinda's supporters. But the king is not for caving in. That was no falsehood, he says, for "it is because of the pole, the axle . . . and the goad that 'chariot' exists as a mere designation." Just so, replies Nagasena, and "Nagasena" exists as a mere designation too, because the five "aggregates" are present. And he quotes the nun Vajira:

> *Just as when the parts are rightly set*
> *The word "chariot" is spoken,*
> *So when there are the aggregates*
> *It is the convention to say "a being."*

The king is impressed, and the chapter ends happily. But just what (you may well ask) have he and Nagasena agreed on? That *chariot*, *self*, *person*, *being*, and *Nagasena* are conventional terms? But aren't *all* words conventional—in England *cow*, in France *vache*, in Poland *krowa*, whatever local convention dictates? Surely they are telling us more than that?

Indeed they are. This is not about the conventionality of language; it is about wholes and their parts, and the point is that wholes are in a sense less real, less objective, and more a matter of convention, than are the parts that compose them. To begin with, the parts are independent in a way that the whole is not: the axle can exist without the chariot existing, but not the chariot without the axle. (As the German philosopher Gottfried Wilhelm Leibniz (1646–1716) said much later, wholes have only a "borrowed" reality—borrowed from the reality of their parts.) Furthermore, what counts as a whole is not given by nature, but depends to some extent on us and our purposes. If from a chariot we remove the pole and one of the wheels, the collection of parts that remains is not incomplete in itself, but only with regard to what we want chariots for.

German philosopher and mathematician Gottfried Wilhelm Leibniz's (1646–1716) statement that wholes have only a borrowed reality, that of their parts, can be seen as a corollary to Buddhist monk Nagasena's challenging argument to King Milinda nearly two thousand years earlier.

But why does all this matter? Why did Nagasena provoke this conversation in the first place? Not just to pass the time, we may be sure. The point is important to him because he holds that what we believe has an effect on our attitudes and through them on our behavior. That, surely, is perfectly reasonable: those, for instance, who believe that the word "God" stands for something real might be expected to feel and perhaps also behave differently from those who think it is just a socially constructed way of speaking. To use the jargon: our metaphysics (what we think reality is fundamentally like) can affect our ethics. Now on the Buddhist view the purpose of philosophy (indeed the purpose of Buddhism) is to alleviate suffering; there is no point in it if it doesn't. And a major cause of suffering is overestimation of the importance of the self, its needs, and its goals: "clinging to self," as Buddhists say. So any change of belief which downgrades the status of the self in our eyes is helpful. A Tibetan text says, "Believing the ego to be permanent and separate, one becomes attached to it; . . . this brings on defilements; the defilements breed bad *karma*; the bad *karma* breeds miseries. . . ." That is why it matters.

Can Nagasena be said to have proved his case in this chapter? Has he really shown that there is no abiding self, just an unstable composite

The purpose of Buddhism is to alleviate suffering, and a major cause of suffering is the overestimation of the importance of the self, so any change of belief that downgrades the importance of the self, as does Nagasena's argument about the parts and the whole, is helpful. In Buddhism, karma is what drives the cycle of suffering and rebirth; the prayer wheel, an example of which is shown here, is used in Buddhism as a way to accumulate wisdom and merit (good karma) and purify negativities (bad karma).

which it is convenient to call a person? Surely not. Even if we accept everything which he and Milinda say about the chariot, it would still have to be argued that the chariot analogy is reliable when it comes to thinking about a person, yet on that point Nagasena says nothing at all. So like most analogies, this one is useful as an illustration or explanation of what the doctrine about the self means, but not as evidence that it is true. Nor do we learn why he gave the crucial answer ("No, sire") to the king's final and crucial question, the one to which a supporter of the permanent self would have said yes: "Is Nagasena apart [distinct] from material form, feeling, perception, mental formations and consciousness?"

So our provisional verdict must be "unproven." But we might ask ourselves whether this question ("Has Nagasena proved his case?") is the right question to be asking. Perhaps it is, if we are trying to make up our minds about the nature of the self; but if we are trying to understand what is going on in the chapter we have been reading, perhaps not. Remember that this is a branch of the tradition that gave us the guru, the authoritative spiritual teacher. In Nagasena's eyes the authority for what he was saying would ultimately be the word of the

Buddha; his own business is to convey the right doctrine in lively and memorable terms. The demand for compelling logic is best reserved for a writer like Hume, to whom it is appropriate because he is genuinely trying to meet it.

Some readers may feel a nagging worry. Buddhists, just as much as Hindus, believe in rebirth—the present Dalai Lama *is* his predecessor, reborn. But if there is no self beyond the five "aggregates," what is there to be reborn, what is it that migrates from one body to the next? How did they reconcile these two doctrines? All I can say here is that they were fully aware of the problem. It leads to a lot more Buddhist metaphysics, which our all-too-brief tour can't even make a start on. But if you have in your hand the edition of *Questions of King Milinda* recommended in the bibliography, turn to pages 58–59 and read the section entitled "Transmigration and Rebirth"—just to begin to get the flavor.

FIVE

Some Themes

●

THE THREE EXAMPLES WE HAVE BEEN LOOKING AT touch on a number of general themes, ideas whose significance goes well beyond that of any single text or for that matter any single school or period. Now I shall pick half a dozen of them out for special attention. To what extent a question can legitimately be considered in abstraction from the particular historical contexts in which it was raised and (perhaps) answered is itself a philosophical question, and no simple one; I shall say something about it in the closing section of the chapter.

Ethical Consequentialism

Don't be frightened by the heading. It is just the trade name of the doctrine that how good or bad something is has to be judged by looking at

Ethical consequentialism is an ethical doctrine in which the value of anything consists in the value of its consequences. The ancient Greek seer Megistias foresaw the consequences of the Battle of Thermopylae: A thousand Greeks, including Megistias, fought the Persians until the last Grecian fell.

its consequences. In *Crito*, as we saw, Socrates was weighing the consequences of the actions open to him, the results for his friends, his children, himself. But there were also considerations about what had happened in the past, not what would result in the future: his past behavior meant that he now had a duty to the state, which required him to accept its judgment and punishment. I suggested at the end of that chapter that if philosophers were going to solve our moral problems they were first going to have to convince us that moral matters are really less complicated than they appear to be. One such attempt is consequentialism: *no* moral reasons are backward looking; proper moral reasons all look to the *consequences* of our actions.

So the idea is that something is good if it has good consequences, bad if it has bad ones. But, you will immediately notice, that doesn't tell us much; we still need to be told which consequences are good ones, which are bad ones. Just repeating the formula (saying: consequences are good when they themselves have good consequences) gets us no further. A consequentialist must be willing to recommend certain things, or states of affairs, as being good *in themselves*. In their case, goodness does not consist in having good consequences—they just are good. Other things are good only to the extent that they lead to them—the things that are good in themselves.

That means that consequentialism isn't any single ethical doctrine, but a general type of doctrine which can take very different specific forms depending on what is held to be good in itself. If you think that the only thing good in itself is pleasure you will live very differently from someone who thinks that the only thing good in itself is knowledge. So even if we could all agree to be consequentialist in our ethical thinking, very little would have been settled.

You might now wonder why we should be so exclusive: why can't lots of different things be good in themselves: pleasure, knowledge, beauty, love—just for starters? That sounds very reasonable. But if what we were hoping for was a moral theory that would make it fairly simple for us to decide what we ought to do, then it is a big step in the wrong direction. Once we agree to take more than one basic value into account we will inevitably find that our values sometimes come into conflict. I might quite often be in a position to promote one value (i.e., do things which have *that* sort of consequence) or another, *but not both*. Which should I choose? If Socrates had had to choose to between risking his friends' lives and damaging his children's education, which should he have chosen?

It is reasonable to wonder why many things can't be good in themselves, such as pleasure and knowledge, or beauty and love, which are personified here in a hand-colored Currier & Ives lithograph from between 1850 and 1910 entitled *The Queen of Love and Beauty*.

How lucky for him that he didn't! What an advantage if we could settle on just one basic value, and measure everything else by the extent to which it leads to that one thing.

No surprise, then, that there have been ethical theories of just that kind. An early one, well worth reading about, is that of Epicurus (341–271 BCE). For him and his followers, the one and only thing valuable in itself was pleasure. But don't expect him to recommend orgies and banquets interspersed with periods of relaxation on the beach of your private island. Because what Epicurus meant by pleasure was not that

Nineteenth-century British philosopher and social reformer John Stuart Mill, shown here in an undated engraving, was somewhat similar to Epicurus in believing that the one thing valuable in itself was happiness, defined as pleasure and the absence of pain.

at all: it was *absence of pain*, both physical and mental. This completely untroubled state, he thought, was as great a pleasure as any. What we immediately think of as pleasures are just different, not more pleasant. This point, and his advice on how to achieve and maintain the ideal state, he appears to have argued for with subtlety and wisdom. I say "appears," because we have very little from his own hand; although he wrote prolifically, our knowledge of him mostly comes from later reports.

A modern and more accessible theory of this type was propounded by John Stuart Mill (1806–73) in his famous essay *Utilitarianism*, where he cited Epicurus as one of his philosophical ancestors. Mill declared the one thing valuable in itself to be happiness—defining it as "pleasure and the absence of pain" (though without holding, as Epicurus had, that the absence of all pain was itself the greatest pleasure). But there is a very significant difference between Mill and Epicurus. For whereas Epicurus seems to have been concerned to advise individuals how best to secure *their own* pleasure/tranquillity, Mill was a social reformer whose ethical principles aimed at the improvement of life (i.e., happiness) for *everybody*. (A similar division is found in the history of Buddhism: is the highest ideal the personal attainment of nirvana, or is it to bring all beings to nirvana, oneself included?) "Let everyone seek to be free from pain and anxiety," says Epicureanism; though it may well add: "Helping those around you to do so will probably help you achieve it too—and if so, help them." For Mill, by contrast, the primary goal is, quite generally, happiness; so anyone else's happiness is just as much your goal as is your own, and any person's happiness is of equal value with anyone else's.

18. ພຸທປະຕິບ ສັງຫາ ທ່ານສົມພານ... ຍອຍຫາງໃຫ້ມະນຸດແລະສັດໄປສູ່ຄວາມສຸຂ ...ສົມມະ ... ພ້ອມດ້ວຍລູກ ບ.ຫ້ວຍຊາຍແກ້ວ

Mill's ethical principles directed him to help all people, not just himself, achieve happiness. In a similar vein, a division in Buddhism asks whether an individual's highest aim is to reach nirvana or to in fact bring all beings, including oneself, to nirvana. This wall painting from a Laotian monastery shows Buddha himself enlightening the path for others to follow so that they can cross the stream of samsara (the endlessly repeating cycle of birth, suffering, and death) to reach nirvana.

Mill's aspirations went beyond his own society—he even writes of improving the condition of the whole of mankind. This was Victorian Britain, and the British Empire pretty much at its zenith (Mill himself worked for the East India Company for over thirty years). But it would be unfair to think of him as an interfering moral imperialist. He didn't want to tell anyone how to be happy; only that everyone should be provided with the material goods, the education and the political and social liberties to work out their own happiness in their own way. Many will find this universality of Mill's basic ethical principle admirable. Some may also wonder whether it can be realistic to ask human beings to spread their moral concern so widely and so impartially. Are we capable of it? And what would life be like if we really tried?

These questions, especially the second, have led some philosophers to think that Mill's doctrine conflicts with another value which nearly all of us regard as very important to us. We have already seen it at work in the *Crito*.

Integrity

One thing that weighed with Socrates, you remember, was the line he had taken at his trial. How could he now choose exile, having explicitly rejected that option when given the opportunity to propose an alternative to the death sentence? "I cannot, now that this fate has befallen me, throw away my previous arguments." As a soldier, he told the court, he had faced death rather than do what was wrong; he will not now do what seems to him to be wrong just to prolong his life.

These thoughts capture a central aspect of the virtue of integrity. Integrity means wholeness, unity; the idea of integrity as a value is the idea of a life lived as a whole rather than as a series of disconnected episodes. So it includes steadfast adherence to principles, and to opinions unless new reasons or evidence appear. Relatedly (and equally applicable to Socrates' case) it includes the value of consistent pursuit of those chosen projects which give purpose and meaning to one's life. And it can also be taken to exclude self-deception and hypocrisy, states in which people are in one way or another at odds with themselves.

So how comfortably does the ideal of integrity fit with Mill's utilitarianism? Not very comfortably at all, some think. For however sincere your commitment to some principle in the past, that fact by itself does not give you—if we take Mill's position seriously and literally—any reason to follow it again now. If in the past your commitment to that principle has consistently led to good effects (measured in terms of happiness), then *that fact* gives you at least some reason to think that it will do so again—which *is* a reason to follow it now. But your commitment to it, however sincere, however much it has become a part of your personality, is not. Critics of utilitarianism question whether we can really live with that way of thinking.

You might like to consider whether utilitarians can defend themselves against that charge. If they can't, things look bad not just for them but for most other types of consequentialist too. For in the last paragraph it wasn't important to think of effects being assessed in terms of happiness; I might have written almost anything instead of "happiness" without affecting the argument. So really this is an attack on consequentialism—of which utilitarianism is only one variety. Anyone who feels that the attack succeeds must accept that the consequences of an action are (at most) only one aspect of its value, and that deciding whether it was right or not may involve a subjective compromise between factors of completely different types.

Political Authority—The Contract Theory

States make demands of their members which would be deeply objectionable if coming from a private person. Tax, for instance. Why is it permissible for the state to appropriate a certain proportion of my income when, if you were even to attempt it, you would be guilty of extortion or "demanding money with menaces"? Or is it just that the state gets away with it—by being easily the biggest menace around?

Now most political theorists hold that the state does have some legitimate authority, though there is less agreement about how much—in other words, about how far this authority can extend while remaining legitimate. Opinions range from totalitarian conceptions, which assign to the state power over all aspects of individuals' lives, to minimalist conceptions, according to which it can do what is necessary to keep the peace and enforce any contracts its members may make with each other, and scarcely anything more. But except for the very few who jump off the bottom end of this scale ("states have no legitimate authority at all"), everyone faces the question how state authority over individuals arises.

An answer with a long history—we have already seen a version of it in *Crito*—is that it arises out of some kind of contract or agreement between individuals and the state of which they are citizens. It is a very natural answer. A person might agree to accept the authority of another (in a certain area of activity) because he saw substantial benefit (for himself) in doing so, and in return for that benefit. Most would accept that such an arrangement legitimates the other's authority over him as far as their agreement reaches, provided that agreement was voluntary. Though natural, it is not the only answer worth considering. Another would be that the stronger has natural authority over the weaker, and this authority is legitimate *so long as* it is used for the weaker's benefit. That might be a good way to think of parents' authority over their infant children, for instance. But if we allow the weaker to be the judges of whether they are benefiting or not, then we are very close to saying that the power is legitimate only so long as they accept it. Whereupon we are back in the neighborhood of a "tacit consent" theory, like the one that the laws and state of Athens appealed to against Socrates (Chapter 2). Unless we allow that superior force makes authority legitimate ("might is right"), or that God has granted authority to certain persons or institutions (the "divine right of kings"), it isn't easy to avoid the contract theory in some form or other.

There are several forms of it because of the wide variety of answers to the question "*Who* makes *what* contract with *whom*?" Since we were speaking of every individual's obligation to the state we might suppose that everyone must individually be a party to the contract (that would appear to be the drift of Socrates' approach in *Crito*); but some theorists write as if it were enough that one's ancestors, or the founders of one's society, should have been party to it. And regardless of that question, is the contract made with the whole of society (so that you contract to go along with the decisions of the whole body, of which you are yourself a member)? Or with some distinct sovereign person or persons to whom you then owe allegiance? You can see that the resulting difference in the constitution may be enormous: anywhere from social democracy to absolute monarchy.

And what is the contract? In what circumstances can the individual properly regard the contract as having lapsed? The famous contract theory of Thomas Hobbes (1588–1679), which we shall return to in Chapter 8, has it that the sole benefit that the contracting individual

THE HOME OF THE AMERICAN CITIZEN AFTER

N.B.—*Scroggs says he is ready and willing to pay any amount of tax, but he*
domestic trifles alone.

BILL HAS PASSED.

...hem to leave his wife's crinoline and other

This cartoon, published in *Frank Leslie's Illustrated Newspaper* on July 19, 1862, shows four tax collectors searching the home of an "American citizen," including under his wife's dress and under the children's bed.

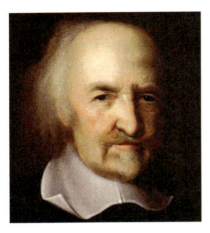

Thomas Hobbes's (1588–1679) famous contract theory states that the sole benefit the contracting individual can rightfully demand from the state is the preservation of his or her life. The English philosopher is shown here in a portrait by seventeenth-century artist John Michael Wright.

can rightfully demand is the preservation of their life: the sovereign puts up a stop to the murderous, thieving lawlessness of the precontractual situation, and organizes defense against attack from without. If that fails, all bets are off; otherwise, complete obedience.

Epicurus had something pertinent to say: "He who knew best how to meet the fear of external foes made into one family all the creatures he could." Even Hobbes granted families a certain natural exemption from the war of all against all. In troubled times families are the groups most likely to hold together, and are the best model for cooperation and allegiance. (Some readers may find that idea out of date—but perhaps that is so because, and in places where, times are easier.) In Plato's prescription for an ideal state (*The Republic*) he in effect abolishes the family—no doubt he had seen much family-centered intrigue and corruption. A plurality of cohesive units within it must be dangerous to the power of the state and its capacity to preserve peace. If there is to be a family it is best that there should only be one—as Epicurus's remark implies—and that the state (recall *Crito* 50e ff.) be thought of as everyone's parent.

The PLEASURES of the MARRIED STATE.

Both Epicurus and Hobbes considered families the most likely to hold together in times of trouble and therefore exempt from the war of all against all. This engraving, printed between 1770 and 1789, shows a family gathered around a table.

Evidence and Rationality

Rationality is what you've got if you have some capacity to reason: to work out, given certain truths, what else is likely to be true if they are; perhaps also (though you need rather more rationality for this) *how* likely. It is the quality of mind Hume was talking about when he said, in *Of Miracles*, that a wise man proportions his belief to the evidence.

Forming the right beliefs, with the appropriate degree of confidence, isn't the only manifestation of rationality, however. A familiar situation is that in which you want to know whether a certain thing is true or not ("Was it the butler who did it?" "Have we any bread in the house?"), and here your rationality will show at least as much in what evidence you seek out, as in what you believe once you have got it.

As well as powers of investigation, we also have a capacity for rational choice: given certain desires, to choose a course of action likely to lead to their fulfillment. And our reason is sometimes, though controversially, assigned a further function: not just to tell us what we ought to do, *given* that we have certain goals, but in addition to tell us what goals we ought to have. There is an influential heavyweight on either side of this tricky question, with Kant affirming that reason does have such a power, Hume denying it. (To my mind Hume and his followers have slightly the better of it, though battle continues.) But here we stick with the issue of belief and evidence.

Why should we be interested in having evidence, or being able to offer reasons, for our beliefs? Because it makes it more likely that they will be true; and it makes us more confident that they are true. Both are important. We want our beliefs to be true, because we use them to direct our actions, and actions directed by true beliefs are on the whole far more successful. (Compare the actions, and the success rate, of two people both wanting a beer: one believes—falsely—that the beer is in the fridge, the other believes—truly—that it is still in the car.) And it helps if we hold our true beliefs confidently, because then we go ahead and act on them, rather than dithering about.

Those are practical considerations, influencing all of us all the time. There may also be theoretical ones, having to do with our philosophical self-image: we (some of us, at certain periods of history) may like to think of ourselves as essentially rational beings in whose lives reason plays an absolutely central role. For a long time philosophers took rationality to be the crucial feature distinguishing humans from other animals. (You can see Hume contesting this view in *Of the Reason of Animals*, the section immediately before *Of Miracles*.)

The idea that reason is absolutely central to human life is a rather vague one, so it isn't the sort of view one could ever prove, or definitively refute, and it would be a bad misjudgment to try. Nevertheless many things can be said that are relevant to it.

The first was well-known to the skeptics of ancient Greece. Suppose you hold some belief (call it B), and you ask yourself what reason you have to hold it. So then you think of some reason (call it R). This R cannot be something you have just dreamed up. You must have a reason to think that *it* is true, if it is to give you a reason for believing B. This further reason can't be B itself, or R again (that would be to give a belief as a reason for itself, which seems like nothing more than reasserting the belief, and is often called "begging the question"), so it must be something else—whereupon the same argument repeats. This suggests that the idea that we have reasons for our beliefs is just a local appearance, which disappears as soon as we try to look at the wider picture: "reasons" turn out to be relative to certain other beliefs for which we have no reasons. The search for a satisfactory response to this argument has structured a whole area of philosophical inquiry known as epistemology or the theory of knowledge.

Add that some of our most basic beliefs, beliefs without which we just couldn't get on with our lives, are very hard to find any decent reason for. A much discussed example is our confidence that things will continue much as they have in the past: your next breath of air won't suffocate you, the floor won't collapse when you take your next step—and hundreds of other things of that kind. With what reason do we believe them? Don't answer: that sort of belief has nearly always worked. True, but that is just another example of what has happened *in the past*, and what we wanted to know was why we expect the future to go the same way.

Without human powers of reasoning—acquiring beliefs by inferring them from previous beliefs—there would be nothing human about us except for the shape of our bodies, and the average chimp would run rings around us. This photograph of a chimpanzee was taken in 1906.

So if the idea was that human belief can be made through and through rationally transparent, or that human life could run on reason alone, then it faces formidable obstacles. But it remains the case that human powers of reasoning, acquiring beliefs by inferring them from previous beliefs, are more than just important to us. Without them there would be nothing recognizably human left except the shape of our bodies, and the average chimp would run rings round us, literally and figuratively.

The Self

Chapter 4 introduced the Buddhist "no-self" doctrine, according to which a person is not a simple, independently enduring thing but a composite, and an easily dissoluble composite at that, of the five "aggregates," which are themselves complex things or states. But that is not the only tradition in which we find the view that a self is really a whole lot of separate things precariously holding together. It appears in the modern West as the so-called bundle theory of the mind, and is almost invariably attributed to Hume. (In your guide's personal opinion it is very doubtful whether Hume actually held it, but I'll skirt round that controversy here.)

So suppose there is some simple, independently enduring thing— you—which just continues the same so long as you exist. Where is it? Look into your own mind and see if you can perceive it. What do you find? In the first place, you notice that you are experiencing a motley of perceptions: visual perceptions of the way your surroundings look, auditory perceptions of the way they sound, perhaps also a few smells, tactual sensations of pressure, roughness, warmth, and suchlike, from touching nearby objects. Then sensations of tension in certain muscles, awareness of bodily movements. All these are continually changing as your position changes and surrounding objects themselves change. You might also feel a slight ache in your foot, or in your forehead; and be aware of a train of thought, perhaps as images or a silent sequence of half-formed sentences. But there is no sign, in this shifting kaleidoscopic complex, of that object "the self," just steadfastly persisting.

Why then suppose that there is such a thing? Well, someone will say, it's clear that all *these* experiences, *my* experiences, somehow belong together; and there are other experiences, those that are not mine but *yours*, which also belong together but don't belong with *this* lot. So there must be one thing, me, my self, which is having all my experiences but isn't having any of yours, and another thing, your self, doing the reverse.

Supporters of the bundle theory reply that nothing of the kind follows. What makes all my experiences hang together doesn't have to be a relation they all stand in to something else; it might be some system of relationships that they all stand in *to each other* (but don't stand in to any of yours). Think of a lot of shreds of paper which form one group by virtue of all being pinned to the same pincushion (the model of the central self)—and a collection of iron filings which form one bunch because they are all magnetized and therefore cling together (the model of the bundle).

You will have noticed the affinity between these thoughts (adapted from Hume, *A Treatise of Human Nature*, book 1, part 4, section 6 [1738]) and those of the Buddhist author from our Chapter 4. But there are also differences, one of the most significant being the status they give to the body. The Buddhist didn't hesitate to include the body ("material form") as one of the five aggregates that compose the person, whereas the eighteenth-century version doesn't even bother to exclude it, but just ignores it completely. Hume writes first "self," then "self or person," then "mind," as if these were obviously the same, so that "What is the self (or person)?" and "What is the mind?" are for him just two ways of asking one question. Such was the change of climate brought about by centuries of religious thought deeply influenced by Plato and Neoplatonism, with their emphasis on the soul and the spiritual and their denigration of the bodily.

There is also another, huge, difference. When presented with a philosophical doctrine it is always a good idea to ask what happens next—that is to say, what its proponents want to do with it. The Buddhists, we saw, had an ethical purpose in mind. The "no-self" theory would help us to live better, keep clear of "defilements," avoid suffering more successfully. Hume's next move was utterly different, having nothing at all to do with ethics but quite a lot to do with what we now call cognitive science. If we do not perceive the enduring self, why then do we believe that we are the same person from day to day? And he proposed a psychological theory to account for it. (It was by today's standards a pretty naive one, but that is only to be expected.)

We are not so much comparing two individuals as two epochs. Nagasena's was the age of survival, Hume's the age of science. Where there is such a difference in the plot, no wonder if a similar thought turns up playing a very different role. Which leads straight into our next topic.

Philosophy and Historical Context

Could Plato and Hobbes, two thousand years apart, with their different backgrounds and circumstances, really have been discussing the same thing? Could a philosopher nowadays be asking the same questions about the self as Hume did, let alone the early Buddhists? Doesn't the idea that we can talk about philosophical themes without reference to whose and when make them sound like timeless objects that thinkers of any epoch can plug into? That view would be quite the opposite of popular nowadays. All thought, we repeatedly hear, is "situated"—tied to the particular historical, social, and cultural circumstances in which thinkers find themselves.

I certainly don't wish to recommend the belief that there are eternal questions just hanging around waiting to be asked. But the view that no question or answer has any existence beyond the specific circumstances of whoever poses it is possibly even worse, and certainly no better. Part of the attraction of such extremes is that they are very simple, somewhat in the pantomime style of "Oh, yes, it is—Oh, no, it isn't." As so often, the truth lies in between and is much more complicated. One can approach this topic in many ways, but I'll choose this way: is it legitimate to treat the thought of someone long since dead as a contribution to a present debate, as if it were being put to us, here and now? I think it is, and that there are even reasons why we should. But it needs to be done with care and—most important—with an eye to what we may be missing.

There is nothing to stop us lifting a sentence from an old text and seeing what it can do for us now. If we want to lift the *thought*, not just the sentence, we may have to put some work into deciding what the sentence meant. If we aren't prepared to do that we shouldn't expect too much of it, and we certainly shouldn't disparage its author if we don't get too much from it. But given that precaution we will often find it relevant to our concerns, because much philosophy arises from facts about human beings and human life which are pretty stable—at any rate they haven't changed much over the last three thousand years.

Finding something relevant is one thing; finding it convincing is another. Suppose we dismiss Plato's and Hobbes's arguments as insufficient to establish the extent of the authority they ascribe to the state. There is something right about this: no doubt their arguments are insufficient. But if we then turn away, taking our business with them to be finished, we risk making a number of mistakes.

One is that though we may have understood what they have written we have not understood *them*—their concerns about what political thought needed, the circumstances that gave rise to these concerns and so made their conclusions attractive to them. So we may be missing the humanity behind the text, and with it an important aspect of what philosophy is for. Furthermore, whenever there is any uncertainty about what they meant, understanding why they were saying it is often a valuable means of resolving the ambiguity. In showing no interest in their motivation we take a risk with our understanding of their words.

A second point is that our appreciation of a philosopher's achievement will be seriously blunted if we do not see the intellectual and emotional circumstances out of which their work grew. I proposed earlier that we think of philosophy as bewildered humankind's attempt to think our way back straight. That is not a story that can be appreciated without some understanding of the circumstances in which thinkers have found themselves.

So "Is this right?" is certainly not the only question we should be thinking about. Still, there is something wrong with refusing altogether to ask whether our philosopher was right, or whether their arguments are convincing, merely because they lived long ago. After all, Plato did not take himself to be writing just for his own time and place. On the contrary, he is constantly trying to direct our attention away from the transient and toward what he believes to be permanent, and it seems deeply condescending (or possibly self-protective?) to dismiss his further ambitions without making any honest attempt to assess them. "There, there, designed his own ideal state, has he?—what a clever little fellow."

I hope that you are now beginning to notice something rather encouraging. The literature of philosophy may be intimidatingly vast, but the number of genuinely distinct philosophical themes is not. It is somewhat too large for the compass of this short book, admittedly, but it is not enormous. We have already seen links across two thousand years between Epicurus and Mill, Plato and Hobbes, Hume and the author of *Milinda*. The problem lies not in becoming familiar with the recurrent themes, but in being sensitive to the variations as different thinkers play them again in their own way for their own purposes. And what this means is that one's understanding of philosophy is cumulative, and accumulates rather quickly. Which must be good news.

THE RIVERSIDE PRESS

HOW CHARMING IS DIVINE PHILOSOPHY.

SIX

Of *Isms*

•

FROM FOOTBALL TO GARDENING and back via cookery, mountaineering, and population genetics, every subject has its own terminology. Philosophy certainly does, most of it fortunately not nearly as frightening as it looks. In Chapter 4 we saw *metaphysics*, meaning the study of (or opinions about) what reality is like in its most general features. In Chapter 5 we encountered *consequentialism*, the blanket word for theories that see the value of anything in its consequences rather than in its own nature and its history; then *epistemology*, the branch of philosophy concerned with knowledge, belief, and closely related notions like reasons and justification. Now let's look at some more words, all of them ending in *ism*. This isn't a matter of cramming for a vocabulary exam—rather of finding out more about philosophy as you learn more of the jargon.

Detail of a mural depicting philosophy by Robert Reid in the Library of Congress Thomas Jefferson Building.

Most philosophical *ism* words are (like *consequentialism*) quite broad terms designating a certain general type of doctrine. Their breadth makes them very flexible, and ensures that they are in constant use, but it also brings dangers, principally that of taking them to say more than they really do. Never think that you have got a philosopher sorted out just because you can say what *ism* he represents. The philosophy of George Berkeley (1685–1752) is a form of idealism, and so is that of Hegel (1770–1831); but I have never heard it suggested that having read either would be any help in understanding the other—their thought is miles apart. Karl Marx (1818–83), on the other hand, certainly wasn't an idealist (which is actually a term of abuse in the Marxist vocabulary), but he is in many respects extremely Hegelian, and that a student should get to know something of Hegel before reading Marx seems the most obvious advice imaginable.

The concept of *isms* is very broad and cannot be relied upon to pigeonhole a philosopher into any particular school of thought. For example, although Karl Marx, shown here in a ca. 1970 Chinese poster, was in no sense an idealist, his philosophy can be far better understood by first acquainting oneself with that of his countryman the avowed idealist Georg Wilhelm Friedrich Hegel.

With that warning uttered and illustrated, let us begin with *dualism*. It can be used of any view which recognizes (exactly) two contrasting forces or entities, so that a theology which posits two basic powers in conflict, one good and one evil, is said to be dualistic.

But by far its most common meaning is a doctrine according to which reality consists of two very different kinds of thing or stuff, namely, mind and matter; a human being consists of a bit of each. Perhaps the most famous exponent of dualism in this sense is the Frenchman René Descartes (some of whose work we shall be looking at in the next chapter). In fact, some enemies of dualism, and there are plenty of them nowadays, seem to want to blame it all on him. (That is historically dubious, to say the least—Descartes was merely trying to give cogent proof of a doctrine that is *very* much older.)

Seventeenth-century French philosopher René Descartes, portrayed here in a statue erected in his honor in La Haye-Descartes, France, was probably the most famous proponent of dualism, the idea that reality consists of two distinct things, namely, mind and matter.

Dualism certainly has its problems, especially if it is to be combined with modern scientific theory. One tricky question is: what does the dualist's mental stuff actually do? We naturally suppose that what we think, what we feel, what we are aware of, affects our behavior. If I *think* that the train leaves in ten minutes, *want* to catch it, and *see* a signpost saying "Railway Station," I will go in the direction I *believe* the signpost points. This means that my (physical) body goes somewhere it wouldn't otherwise have gone. But doesn't scientific theory suggest that all physical events have other physical events as their causes? In which case how can there be room for something *else*, of a nonphysical kind, to cause my body to move? Dualists may just have to grit their teeth and say that science is plain wrong about that. For if they agree that science is right on that point, and if they agree (and it would be weird not to) that what we think, feel, and so forth affects what we do, then the consequence is that thinking, feeling, awareness, and so on must be *physical* processes. In which case the question comes round again: what does this nonphysical stuff of theirs, this "mind," actually do? But dualists can't *just say* that science is wrong about all physical events having physical causes. That won't convince anyone who wasn't convinced to start with. They will need some reason for saying that there is something about us which cannot be physical. When we come to Descartes we'll see something of what a dualist might have to offer on that score.

So, you may be thinking, if dualism is the view that there are two ultimate sorts of stuff, mind and matter, probably we also find a doctrine that says there is only matter, and another that holds that there is nothing but mind. And you're quite right. The first is called *materialism*, the second *idealism* (not mentalism), and both have plenty of history.

The earliest materialism of which we have clear record is that of the Indian Lokāyatas, often known as Cārvākas after one of their most eminent thinkers (incidentally, pronounce *c* in these Sanskrit words as *ch*). Remember them if you find yourself slipping into the common error of imagining that all Indian philosophy is mystical, religious, and ascetic. Only perception confers knowledge, and what you can't perceive doesn't exist, they reckoned. The eternal soul that, as the Brahmins suppose, passes on from life to life, is a fiction. You have one life and one only—try to enjoy it. The movement appears to have survived for over a thousand years; unfortunately, just about all we now know of it comes from reports written by its opponents.

In Greece Democritus—a fairly close contemporary of Socrates—propounded a theory which, until twentieth-century physics changed the picture, sounded very modern: the universe consists of myriads of very

Democritus, a Greek contemporary of Socrates', held that the universe is made up of very small particles called atoms moving in a vacuum or void. Also known as the laughing philosopher, Democritus is shown in a 1628 oil on panel by Dutch artist Hendrik ter Brugghen.

small material particles moving in a vacuum or void. These little things are called "atoms" (from the Greek for uncuttable or indivisible); they and the void they move through are literally everything there is. This rather good guess was taken over by Epicurus (we've seen him already) and his school, but the easiest place to read about it is in a famous work by Lucretius, a Roman admirer of Epicurus, called "Of the Nature of Things" (or "Of the Nature of the Universe"—depending on which translation you have got hold of).

You might expect materialism to be completely incompatible with any sort of religious belief—as the case of the Lokāyatas appears to confirm. But watch out for surprises! The Epicureans believed in gods, but then held (as consistency demanded) that they had bodies made of a very refined type of matter. (They live somewhere a very long way from here in a state of divine bliss and untroubled happiness—paying not a wink of attention to human life. Opponents said this was just a way of being atheists without admitting it.)

The word *materialism* as it occurs in everyday usage is rather different. A "material girl" isn't a girl who consists of matter only—though if philosophical materialists are right that is all she consists of, and so does the material world she lives in. But the everyday "materialism" which some bemoan and others just enjoy isn't wholly unrelated to the philosophers' sort. Madonna's material girl derives her pleasures mostly from material objects—their ownership and consumption—in preference to the pleasures of the mind. Everyday materialism is the attachment to what is—now in the philosophers' sense—material, as opposed to what is spiritual or intellectual. The philosophy of Marx came to be called dialectical materialism, not so much because he held that there is literally nothing but matter as because he held that the most important underlying causes in human life are material: economic facts about the way in which a society produces its material goods. (What "dialectical" meant we shall see in Chapter 7 when we encounter Hegel.)

Idealism is also a word with an everyday as well as a technical meaning. At the technical end it is applied to views that deny the existence of matter and hold that everything there is, is mental or spiritual, like that of the Irish bishop George Berkeley, whom we mentioned earlier. Someone who tells us that had better explain, in the next breath, what then are these things like chairs and mountains that we keep bumping into and falling off. When he heard it said that Berkeley could not be refuted, the celebrated man of letters Dr. Johnson is reputed to have answered: "I refute him thus," and kicked a stone. But refuting Berkeley isn't that easy. (I use the word *refute* to mean *showing* that something is wrong, not just *saying* that it is wrong—which of course is very easy indeed and can be done by anyone, especially someone like Dr. Johnson, who was rarely short either of an opinion or of a memorable way of expressing it.)

Perhaps Berkeley can be refuted, but only if we can somehow overcome the following well-worn line of thought. What I am really aware of when I look at a table is not the table itself but *how the table looks to me.*

Irish philosopher Bishop George Berkeley (1685–1753) believed that everything that there is, is mental or spiritual. The bishop is shown here in an image from around 1740.

"How it looks to me" describes not the table, but my mind—it is the state of consciousness which the object, whatever it is, produces in me when I look at it. And this goes on being true however closely, or from however many angles, I look at the table; and it goes on being true if I *touch* the table—except that then the object (whatever it is) produces a different kind of state of consciousness in me, tactual sensations as opposed to visual. If I kick the table (or Dr. Johnson's stone) and it hurts, that is yet another state of my consciousness. Admittedly, these states of consciousness fit together very nicely; we quickly learn from a very few of them to predict quite accurately what the rest are going to be like—one glance, and we know pretty much what to expect. But the table itself, the physical table, isn't so much an established fact as a *hypothesis* that explains all these states of perceptual consciousness. So it might be wrong—some other hypothesis might be the truth. Berkeley himself thought precisely that, though partly because he believed he had proved that the very idea of a nonmental existent was incoherent. (I'm not going to trouble you with his supposed proof here.) Believing as he did in a benevolent and all-powerful god, he made his will the direct cause of our states of consciousness and declared matter redundant—as well as incoherent.

Hume—again—made a nice comment. Berkeley's arguments, he said, "admit of no answer and produce no conviction." However impossible we may find it to believe Berkeley's denial of matter, a convincing proof that he just *couldn't* be right has been extremely elusive. I myself don't believe that there is one—though neither, you won't be surprised to hear, do I believe Berkeley.

Some philosophical systems (like Hegel's) qualify as idealism not because they deny the very existence of matter but because they regard it as subordinate to the mental or spiritual, which is what really determines the nature of reality and gives it purpose. This use of *idealism* parallels the use of *materialism* we noticed above, in its application to the philosophy of Karl Marx. But when we come to the everyday notion of idealism the parallel with *materialism* fails. A materialist's attention is fixed on material goods as opposed to mental, spiritual, or intellectual ones; whereas an idealist is not someone always focused on the latter rather than the former, but someone committed to *ideals*. And ideals are essentially *things of the mind*, because they are the thoughts of circumstances not in fact found in reality, but which we can strive to approach as nearly as the conditions of life permit. The mental nature of ideals makes the connection between the everyday usage of the word and the technical one.

Two more *isms* of which one hears a lot, and which tend to occur together as a pair of supposed opposites, are *empiricism* and *rationalism*. Whereas *dualism*, *materialism*, and *idealism* belong to metaphysics (what sorts of thing are there?), this pair belongs squarely to epistemology (how do we know?).

In a rough-and-ready way we all make a distinction between perceiving and thinking. It is one thing to see the objects on your table, notice that one is a pen and one a computer; it is another thing to think about them, wonder if they still work, or what to do if they don't. And we are used to the idea that astronomers spend long hours looking at the sky, whereas mathematicians just seem to sit there working things out, feeling no need to look at anything at all except what they themselves have written down. So here, on the face of it, are two quite different ways of acquiring knowledge. Some philosophers have favored one of them at the expense of the other: *empiricism* is a very general word for doctrines that favor perceiving over thinking, *rationalism* for doctrines that favor thinking over perceiving.

There may have been philosophers who held that only what could be perceived could be known, so allowing no cognitive powers at all to thought, inference, and reason. Something of much that kind is reported of the Lokāyatas, whom we met above in connection with materialism. According to some reports of their thinking they went even further, saying that only what can be perceived exists. If so (but remember that all the reports we have were written by their opponents!), they surely overreached themselves. Nobody who thinks that knowledge is only of what you have perceived can claim to know that nothing imperceptible exists, since that isn't something you could possibly perceive. (It would make as much sense as claiming to be able to *hear* that nothing inaudible exists.)

An empiricist who holds that only perception yields knowledge need not be saying that the process of perception itself involves no thought whatever, so that we can have as it were pure perception untainted by

Empiricism is a general word used to describe doctrines that favor perceiving over thinking as a source of knowledge, whereas rationalism favors thinking over perceiving. This etching by T. G. Flowers, showing two men engaged in empirical and rational analysis, appeared in Denison Olmstead's *Mechanism of the Heavens*, originally published in the mid-1800s.

any thinking. Even to look at my table and see that there is a pen on it requires more of me than just passively registering the light patterns that enter my eyes. I need to know a little about pens, at the very least about what they look like, and then bring this knowledge to bear, otherwise I shall no more *see a pen* than does the camera with which we photograph the pen. Perception is interpretative, whereas cameras merely record patterns of light. So a less crude empiricism will allow that classification, thought, inference, and reason all have their legitimate role. But it will take its stand on the point that they cannot generate a single item of knowledge on their own. It may be true that there is no thought-free perception; but it is also true that there is no perception-free knowledge. All claims to knowledge answer, in the end, to perception; it may be possible for them to go beyond perception, but they must start from it.

The empiricist can offer a powerful argument for this view; any would-be rationalist must have an answer ready. In perception we are in some kind of contact with objects around us; they have an effect on our senses. But if we try to think in complete independence of perception, where is the link between us and the objects we are trying to think about? For if there is no such link, then there is the world, and here are we thinking away to ourselves. That sounds like a recipe for pure fantasy, perhaps interspersed with the very occasional lucky guess. Let us take a quick look at how three philosophers of strongly rationalist tendencies, Plato, Kant, and Hegel, responded to this challenge.

What reason can tell us, according to Plato, is not directly about the world of the senses at all, but about eternal, transcendent entities called Ideas or Forms: the Good, the Just, the Equal, the Beautiful. Things we perceive with the senses are good, equal, and so on just insofar as they "participate" in these Forms or approximate to the standards set by them. But how does

According to Plato, shown here in an illustration from the *Nuremberg Chronicle*, reason tells us about eternal, transcendent entities, not directly about the world of the senses.

reason get its knowledge of the Forms? Plato (as you will know by now if you took my advice to read his *Phaedo* as a follow-up to *Crito*) made use of a belief far from unknown to ancient Greek thought. The soul has existed before it entered its present body. In that existence it encountered—Plato hints obscurely at something analogous to perception—the Forms, and in rational thought it is now brought to remember what it then learned of them.

Kant, who was happy to concede far more to empiricism than Plato or Hegel, met the challenge in a novel and radical way. Reason cannot tell us anything about things imperceptible—it can only tell us what, in general terms, our experience is bound to be like. And it can do this only because *our experience is shaped by our own minds*. Reason, operating on its own, is really only telling us how our minds work—which is why it can do what it does without needing to draw on our perceptions of the rest of the world.

Hegel's response is not unlike Plato's, in that he begins with a system of thoughts or universals which he collectively calls "the Idea." This is the driving force which structures the whole of reality, which includes our minds and the categories in which we think, as well as the rest of reality, which is what we are thinking about. That is why we can expect our reason, even when used on its own independently of perception, to be in tune with the world. The reasoning subject and its object share a structure, that of the Idea.

Immanuel Kant, shown here in a marble sculpture from 1798 by Emanuel Bardou, believed that reason could show us only what, in general terms, our experience was bound to be like, not about things that were imperceptible.

These three examples show us that the opposition between empiricism and rationalism is not a minor skirmish. Those who begin by taking opposite sides at this point can end up worlds apart, metaphysically speaking. But I do not mean to suggest that only rationalism faces difficulties and empiricism is problem free. Not so, as we shall soon find out.

Another much-used *ism* is *skepticism*. One can be skeptical, of course, about specific things like the probity of the Olympic Committee, the existence of UFOs, or the value of a low-fat diet, but when *skepticism* occurs in philosophical texts it usually refers to something much more general: the rejection of a wide range of claims to knowledge, or doubts about a large class of beliefs. It isn't just their number, of course. Any skepticism worthy of a place in the history books must be aimed at beliefs that are actually held, and are held to be important—no medals are awarded for shelling the desert.

This means that there can be plenty of thought which was skeptical in its own time, but now reads differently. A good example would be *Quod nihil scitur* (*That Nothing Is Known*), by the Portuguese philosopher-medic Francisco Sanchez (1551–1623). A more skeptical-sounding title it would be hard to find, but what follows seems to us not so much skepticism as a vigorous attack on Aristotelianism, then prevalent but now long since discredited. When skeptics succeed they cease to look like skeptics; they look like critics who were right.

Other forms of skepticism have a longer shelf life. These are the ones whose targets are perennial human beliefs, or everyday beliefs, or what is often called common sense. The most famous example of modern times occurs at the beginning of Descartes's *Meditations*, where we are threatened with the possibility that the senses cannot be relied upon to tell us anything whatever about the world, not even that there is one. But Descartes is on the program for the next chapter, so let us here look back instead to the school of Pyrrho (roughly 365–275 BCE), source of the most developed skeptical philosophy we know. It can all be found in a single book, *Outlines of Pyrrhonism*

German philosopher Georg Wilhelm Friedrich Hegel believed that the reasoning subject and its object shared a universal structure, that of the "Idea." Hegel is pictured here in one of a set of German stamps that was created to mark the two hundredth anniversary of the philosopher's birth.

by Sextus Empiricus. Sextus, in his prime around 200 CE, here reports in loving detail the aims, arguments, and conclusions of the system. Happy the movement that finds a chronicler like him.

The early pyrrhonists had worked hard. They had catalogued ten "tropes," or ways of arguing for their skeptical conclusion that we have no sufficient grounds for any conviction as to what things are really like, as opposed to how they appear to us. Faced with a "dogmatist"—one of the politer names they called people like Aristotelians and Stoics who claimed to know such things—their favorite strategy was to

Greek physician and philosopher Sextus Empiricus (ca. 160–ca. 210 CE) documented the aims, arguments, and conclusions of the school of Pyrrho, the source of the most developed skeptical philosophy we know.

find some animal to which things would appear differently, or other human beings to whom they appeared differently, or circumstances under which they would appear differently to the claimants themselves, and then to argue that there was no way of resolving the disagreement without arbitrarily favoring one viewpoint over the rest. In one passage Sextus argues that there is no reason to privilege the way something seems to a dogmatist over the way it seems to a dog. Readers will occasionally catch him arguing from premises which a skeptic might be expected to find untrustworthy. Perhaps he, and the pyrrhonists, were not always speaking to eternity, but to their contemporaries—and felt that what *they* accepted could legitimately be used against them.

Nowadays one often hears it asked what the point of a comprehensive skepticism could be—asked rhetorically, with the implication that it can have no point whatever. But the pyrrhonists certainly thought that their skepticism had a point: the achievement of tranquillity of mind, untroubledness, *ataraxia*. They knew a thing or two about peace of mind. If you want to insist on the truth of your point of view, remember that there is a cost: life is going to be a perpetual intellectual brawl. And if the brawl stays intellectual, you'll have been lucky; especially in religion and politics, these things have been known to end in bombs and burnings.

I think they knew something else as well: moving from how things immediately appear to our senses to what they are really like is a much slower, more hazardous and laborious enterprise than many of their contemporaries realized.

The pyrrhonists' favorite skeptical maneuver was to remind us that how a thing appears does not just depend on the thing: it depends on the condition of the person *to whom* it appears, and the medium *through which* it appears. Which ushers in our final *ism*: *relativism*. Relativism is not a specific doctrine, but a type of doctrine—I might add, a type much in vogue with intellectuals at the moment. The general idea is easy to grasp. A moral relativist will hold that there is no such thing as good (pure and simple), rather there is good-in-this-society, good-in-that-society. An aesthetic relativist rejects the idea that an object might simply be beautiful; we always have to ask, "Beautiful for whom, in whose eyes?" A "gastronomic relativist" won't be interested in the question whether pineapple tastes nice—it has to be "tastes nice to whom, when, and in combination with what?" A literary relativist doesn't believe that texts have meanings—except at best in the sense that they have a variety of meanings for a variety of readers, and probably even for one reader at different times. A relativist about rationality will say that what is rational is relative to cultures, with the consequence (for instance) that it is illegitimate to apply "Western" scientific standards to traditional African beliefs about witchcraft and pronounce them irrational.

That bunch of examples illustrates a number of points about relativism. One is that the initial plausibility of different cases of relativism varies widely. Many people will find aesthetic relativism easily acceptable, and some will think that what I have called "gastronomic relativism" is *obviously* true. That rationality is culture relative is a much more difficult doctrine, as is relativism about moral values. These doctrines do not say, remember, that different beliefs are *accounted* rational in different societies, and different moral values *avowed*, for this nobody doubts. They say that what these *really are* can differ from society to society, and that is about as far from obvious as you can get. So if you hear someone going on about relativism without saying relativism *about what*, give a badly concealed yawn.

The examples illustrate another important point. It isn't just what the particular relativism is about; it is also what it relativizes to: the individual, a society, a culture (there are plenty of multicultural societies), a historical epoch, or what. Those forms of relativism, like the "gastronomic," which can plausibly focus on the individual, have a big advantage: unlike societies, cultures, and epochs, it is clear where an individual begins and ends. If Europeans shouldn't bring their scientific standards to bear on African beliefs in witchcraft, may they properly bring them to bear on European beliefs in witchcraft? Or only on *contemporary* European beliefs in witchcraft? Imagine yourself living intermingled with a people who, routinely and without moral qualms, abandon unwanted babies and leave them to die. (Such societies have existed.) Could you just say "Oh, fine. That's what they think, that's their moral culture, ours is different," as if it were like "They speak French and we speak English"? Bitter experience suggests that many people are unlikely to find it that easy.

I would be a bad guide if I left you with the impression that a short paragraph can dispose of moral and intellectual relativism, just like that. Be aware, though, that in several areas relativism is in for a rough ride. The ride is rough theoretically, because of the difficulty of stating clearly just what relativism does and doesn't say; and it is rough practically, because of the difficulty of standing by it when the crunch comes.

When it comes to relativism, it isn't just what the particular relativism is about; it is also what it relativizes to: the individual, a society, a culture, for example. If Europeans shouldn't bring their standards to bear on African witchcraft, can they do so on European witchcraft, or only on contemporary European witchcraft? This engraving, created around 1505, of a witch riding backward on a goat and accompanied by four putti is by German painter and engraver Albrecht Dürer (1471–1528).

SEVEN

Some More High Spots:
A Personal Selection

●

IN CHAPTERS 2, 3, AND 4 WE LOOKED CLOSELY at three pieces of philosophical writing. In this chapter I briefly introduce a few more of my favorites. The selection is personal—another author would very likely have made quite different choices. And it can only be a few. But be assured that there are plenty more, indeed that however much you read, there will *still* be plenty more.

Descartes: *Discourse on the Method*

In Chapter 2 I remarked that, whereas the ethical discussion presented in Plato's *Crito* could almost have taken place yesterday, Plato's cosmology

Different authors favor different philosophical writings, and there is a wide variety from which to choose. The poster *Dig* (ca. 1909) is by Sadie Wendell Mitchell.

takes us back to a completely different world. True—but we needn't go back that far; four centuries will be enough. In 1600 it was, admittedly, over fifty years since Copernicus had offered his replacement for the old Ptolemaic astronomy, moving the sun to the center of the solar system and letting the Earth, now just one of a number of similar planets, circle around it. But few believed him. Galileo (1564–1642) had not yet begun publicly to champion his cause, and when he did so by no means everybody believed *him*.

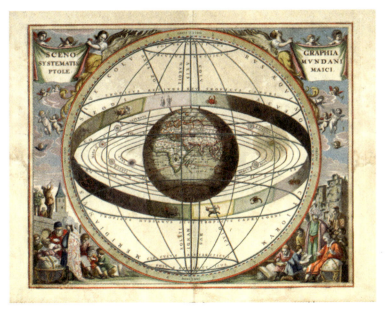

Two thousand years of history, represented by the accepted wisdom of Aristotelian physics and cosmology, began to crumble during the Scientific Revolution. Copernicus's astronomy challenged that of Ptolemy, and Copernicus's advances were soon to be championed by Galileo. This portrayal of the Ptolemaic system, showing the signs of the zodiac and the solar system with the Earth at its center, was published in the *Harmonia Macrocosmica Andreas Cellarius* (1660–61) by J. van Loon.

It was not just that the Earth was displaced from its proud position in the center. In fact it wasn't really that at all, since according to what we would now call the physics of the day the center was not a very desirable place to be: it was where the basest matter tended to congregate, the cosmic rubbish bin, one might almost say. Other factors were far more important. Passages in the Bible appear to maintain that the Earth is stationary; here was an individual prepared to reject or at least reinterpret those passages on the basis of his own reasoning without reference or deference to proper authority. Besides, the claims made by Copernicus, let alone Galileo, were in conflict with the (neo-Aristotelian) physics and cosmology that held sway in the universities.

For an Aristotelian, the baser kinds of matter are earth and water. Unlike the other two kinds, air and fire, they naturally strive toward the center of the universe. So a spherical mass of earth and water has formed there, and this is the Earth. (However often you hear it said, it just isn't true that the medievals believed that the Earth was flat!) But the Moon, the Sun, the planets, and stars don't consist of this sort of matter at all, not even air and fire. They are made of the Quintessence—the fifth element—incorruptible and unchanging, and all they do is go around in circles, eternally, in godlike serenity. Now the new astronomy wants to blow this distinction away: however things may look and feel from where we are standing, the Earth is itself in the heavens; and the heavenly bodies are not utterly set apart, but are as much proper objects of scientific investigation as the Earth itself. On top of which the new scientists want to replace explanations couched in terms of natures and goals with talk of the particles of which things are composed, and of mechanical causation governed by mathematical laws.

All this represented catastrophic intellectual change on several levels at once. It is often called the Scientific Revolution, a name which captures its magnitude, but wrongly suggests that it happened quickly. No wonder that it was accompanied by a rise of skepticism. For if the best of received wisdom, with two thousand years of triumphant history, was now seen to be failing, a natural reaction was to despair of human knowledge altogether and call off the hunt.

René Descartes (1596–1650) viewed Aristotelianism as a time-hallowed system of errors. So did the skeptics, but unlike them he also took it to be an obstacle—an obstacle to human knowledge of nature, like skepticism itself. So he conceived an ambitious plan. (Had he known just *how* ambitious he might have stopped in his tracks there and then—so we should be grateful that he didn't.) By going back to a point at which no doubt was even possible and then rebuilding human knowledge by unmistakable steps, he would fight his way clear of skepticism, and presumably of Aristotelianism as well, since

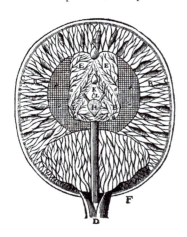

Part of Descartes's journey to rebuild human knowledge included advances in the sciences. Shown here is the philosopher's diagrammatic drawing of a section of human brain, which appeared in his *Treatise of Man* (1664), published posthumously, having been withdrawn from publication when the church condemned Galileo.

Descartes's *Discourse* on the Method of Rightly Using One's Reason (1637) provides a taste of most of the author's thought, including an autobiographical account of why he undertook his daunting project in the first place.

he had no expectation that his reconstruction would lead back in that old, worn, faltering direction. Then he would illustrate the value of this heroic Great Escape of the human intellect by demonstrable progress in the sciences: optics, physics, physiology, and meteorology were all topics that he wrote about.

The *Discourse on the Method of Rightly Using One's Reason* (1637) is not Descartes's most famous work—that title surely goes to his *Meditations* (1641). But it has the advantage of giving the reader, in very brief compass, a taste of most of Descartes's thought, including very importantly an autobiographical account of the circumstances and motivation from which his whole project arose.

So set aside a couple of hours—easily enough—and begin by sympathizing with Descartes's frustration when formal education left him feeling that "I had gained nothing . . . but increasing recognition of my ignorance" and that there was "no such knowledge in the world as I had previously been led to hope for." Admittedly, there is value in some of what he has been taught, and he gives a sentence each to the advantages of languages, history, mathematics, oratory, and poetry—though the latter two are "more gifts of the mind than fruits of study." As for philosophy, its chief "advantage" is that it enables us to "speak plausibly about any subject and win the admiration of the less learned"—so much for scholastic Aristotelianism. So the minute he is old enough he chucks it all in and goes traveling, joining in the wars which were boiling away in Europe at this time. Perhaps men of action will have more truth to offer than the scholars; after all, their misjudgments really do rebound on them, whereas those of the scholars have no practical consequences and can be false with impunity.

One thing he learns on his travels is how much customs differ from place to place, people to people—as he pointedly says, there is as much variety as in the opinions of the philosophers—so he had better not rely on anything he has learned only through "custom and example." At this stage many people (and nowadays even more than then) might slip into a forlorn skepticism or a lazy relativism. But not this one. Descartes's reaction is that if he is to avoid living under the misguidance of false opinions, then once in his life he should dismantle his entire belief system and construct it anew. Which he intends to try—and on his own what's more.

One has to be amazed at the audacity of this unflinchingly positive response to the crisis that Descartes, doubtless along with many less articulate or less self-confident contemporaries, was experiencing. If, that is, we believe that he really meant it—but I know no good reason to think that he didn't. In Part 2 of the *Discourse* we see him striving to reassure any readers who may take him for a social, political, or theological reformer: "No threat to any public institution, it's only my own beliefs that I'm going to overhaul." (Prudent, and a nice try, but not altogether convincing, is it? As if he weren't going to recommend his renovated belief system to anyone else!) Then in Part 3 he takes steps to ensure that his life can keep ticking over while his beliefs are suspended, for "before starting to rebuild your house you must provide yourself with somewhere to live while building is in progress." So he will simply go along, noncommittally, with the most sensible and moderate views and behavior he finds around him. It is a modified version of what he would have found in Sextus Empiricus's report of the recommendations of the ancient skeptics—who faced the same problem permanently, since they had no intention of rebuilding.

How is demolition to proceed, and where will Descartes find his foundations? At the start of Part 4 he suddenly feigns to go all shy: perhaps he should bypass this bit, as being "too metaphysical and uncommon for everyone's taste." But then he tells us anyway. What we get in Part 4 is a high-speed résumé of his best-known work, the *Meditations on First Philosophy*.

First, suspend any belief about which you can think of the slightest grounds for doubt. (Don't bother about whether these grounds actually do make you *feel doubtful*—mostly they won't, but that could just be a fact about you.) Since your senses have sometimes deceived you, consider the possibility that they might deceive you at any time, indeed that they might deceive you *all* the time—that they have no more status than a dream or a hallucination. But what about your belief that you are now thinking? Here doubt really does run dry, because doubting whether you are thinking is another case of thinking—the doubt defeats itself. And if I am thinking, Descartes reflects, then I must exist—we have reached the notorious *Cogito ergo sum*.

You may well wonder how Descartes is to rebuild anything on the basis of what little has survived so fierce a test. But he isn't cowed by the task. He has found that his grasp of his own existence is absolutely secure. But he can raise doubts about everything else, even his own body.

So he (his mind, soul, self) must be something else, distinct from his body, and capable of existing without it. The body is one thing, the mind another—this is the famous (or infamous) Cartesian dualism that we saw in Chapter 6.

In the next step Descartes observes that he has the idea of a perfect being, God, so the question arises: how did he get the ability to think such a thought? As he points out elsewhere, if you had in mind the plan of an extremely intricate machine we would think that either you were a superb engineer yourself or had got the plan from someone who was. And since Descartes knows that he is far from perfect himself, he reckons his idea of a perfect being can't come from him, but only from a being that is actually perfect. That idea in his mind is the signature left by his creator.

Many readers will feel that Descartes's idea of a perfect being is far too hazy, imprecise, and in a word *imperfect* to need anything more than Descartes for its cause. But he held the existence of God to be proved, and took a further step: what he believes when he has achieved the utmost clarity of which he is capable must be true. For otherwise his God-given faculties would be misleading in principle, which would make God a deceiver, and hence imperfect. So if skepticism says that even our very best efforts might lead us to falsehood, just dismiss it.

In Part 5 we are back with autobiography. Descartes turns to his scientific work, things which he had earlier "endeavoured to explain in a treatise which certain considerations prevent me from publishing." These "considerations" were in fact the condemnation of Galileo's writings by the church, as Descartes makes clearer (though without mentioning names) in Part 6. There he offers reasons for

Italian astronomer and physicist Galileo Galilei is shown here in a 1636 portrait by Flemish artist Justus Sustermans.

his decision, and for his further decision to present some of his results in the *Discourse* after all. The reasons are fairly convoluted, and don't wholly dispel the suspicion that the case of Galileo had just frightened him off.

At this stage one of those unfortunate little things happens. Descartes was a notable mathematician, and no mean performer in physics. True, the work of Isaac Newton (1642–1727) wiped his physics off the map toward the end of the century, though not before Newton himself had accepted it and attempted to work within it until his late thirties. But the main example he selects for Part 5 is his theory about how the human heart works, and this nowadays sounds just plain quaint and fanciful—he believes it to be much hotter than any other part of the body, and makes it sound like a distillery in action. (All it distills is blood, some readers may be disappointed to learn.)

In spite (or partly because) of this glitch, the *Discourse* is a rich and memorable work. An eminent founder of modern thought grapples with himself, Aristotelianism, skepticism, academic reaction, public and ecclesiastical opinion, physics, cosmology, and physiology, all in about fifty pages. Now that I call a real feast.

Hegel: *Introduction to the Philosophy of History*

We encountered Georg Wilhelm Friedrich Hegel (1770–1831) in Chapter 6, though only briefly. His influence has been massive; we shall see two examples of it in the next and final chapter, but important as they are they can give only the barest inkling of the extent of the Hegel phenomenon. And the opposition to him started two very significant movements: existentialism, through the Danish thinker Søren Kierkegaard, and in Britain the analytic school through Moore, Bertrand Russell, and the young Ludwig Wittgenstein. It took heavyweights with an alternative on offer to take people's minds off Hegel, and then the effect was only partial, local, and temporary.

Georg Wilhelm Hegel's thought in the *Philosophy of History* begins not with ordinary, everyday considerations but with a grand vision of reality and the forces that move it. The German philosopher is shown here in his study in a lithograph by Ludwig Julius Sebbers from 1828.

Nineteenth-century Danish philosopher Søren Kierkegaard, memorialized here in a statue in the Royal Library Gardens, Copenhagen, opposed Hegel's theories.

But there is another reason for introducing a work by Hegel at this point. Nearly all the philosophy we have looked at so far begins from what are relatively ordinary, everyday considerations. (Socrates: what will happen to my children if I do what my friends are suggesting? Hume: you can't always believe what other people tell you. Descartes: when there's so much disagreement between the authorities, what can we do but go back to basics and start again?) Hegel's thought in the *Philosophy of History*, in contrast, arises out of a grand vision of reality and the forces that move it—this is heavy-duty metaphysics.

Hegel is often said to be a very difficult philosopher. I won't deny it—if you select a page at random and read it from top to bottom you will probably feel that you might just as well have read it from bottom to top. But one of the most valuable experiences for someone coming new to his philosophy is that of finding how much easier things are if you approach the text with the grand metaphysical vision already in mind. The big picture is the key, so we begin by trying to get some grasp of it. Remember that I warned you back in Chapter 1 to expect to find some philosophy weird. You will find Hegel's less weird, even if you still don't believe a word of it, after you have read the *Introduction to the Philosophy of History*. Here goes.

We start with something called "the Idea." Think of it as being rather like the Ideas of Plato—a system of abstract universals from which things and events in the world take their shapes and natures. But it differs from Plato in two important ways. First, it is a highly structured system, and its structure is in a certain sense *developmental*. I say "in a certain sense" because the Idea doesn't happen in time, one bit after another; Hegel's doctrine is rather that it embodies a natural order of thought, so that the thought of one element inexorably leads the mind to another, and the thought of those two to a third, and so on until the whole system is revealed.

The second big difference is that whereas Plato speaks as if his Ideas exist independently of anything else, Hegel's Idea can exist only if something embodies it. So there has to be "Nature"—the familiar collection of concrete objects that surround us. And Nature, since it exists in order to embody the Idea, reflects all the Idea's properties. The "development," which in the Idea was metaphorical, makes a literal appearance in the changing patterns of Nature.

So the Idea and Nature are very closely related: each is a form of the other. But at the same time they are so different that you might well think of them as opposites. The Idea is abstract, and neither temporal nor spatial, whereas Nature is spatio-temporal and concrete. The Idea is composed of universals, general concepts, whereas Nature comprises myriads of particular things. And it is material, which the Idea is certainly not. Hegel now uses this situation—the existence of opposites which are nevertheless in a sense the same thing—as the starting point for a deeply characteristic move.

Suppose that you want to know something about yourself, say, what you really think about some question or other. Should you sit down meditatively and try to introspect your own thoughts? No—you will just think you see whatever you wanted to see. You should do something, make something, write something, in general produce *something that expresses you*, your own work—and look at it. That is what will tell you about yourself.

Good advice, and nothing especially new. ("By our works shall we know ourselves.") But Hegel now makes a very surprising (and rather obscure) use of

Meissen porcelain figurine of a woman writing (1772).

it. He holds, remember, that Nature is the concrete expression of the Idea. So the Idea is confronted by *its own work*, and the situation is ripe for it to start to understand itself. Thus is born what Hegel calls *Geist*, usually translated "spirit"—consciousness, awareness. Human minds are its vehicle, but what is really happening in them is that the Idea is gradually moving toward full self-understanding. (OK, I told you that this was my example of high-altitude metaphysics!) There's more to come: Hegel believes that the whole purpose of reality is precisely this, that the Idea should come to full knowledge of its own nature. And this is to happen in us, in the minds of the human race. No philosopher has ever cast us in a more prestigious role. Indeed, could there be one? This is the high-water mark of human self-assessment.

So what of history? History begins only when there are conscious beings and something one might call a culture, that is to say when we have reached Hegel's Stage 3—Spirit or *Geist*. History is driven by Reason, the Idea: Hegel makes no bones of announcing this as established fact, something which philosophy (his own philosophy) has shown. In history, the Idea is working out its rational purposes.

If you find this thought rather alien, remember that to most of Hegel's audience it would have sounded quite familiar; it is a close relative of something they had been brought up to accept. Providence is at work. Behind all the mundane detail of life, God is realizing his aims. In spite of everything, Good is gradually defeating Evil. All is for the best. That thought is familiar to all of us, including those of us who snort at it. What makes Hegel's version of it feel unfamiliar is, first, his conception of "the best"—the Idea, the force that drives it all, comes to full knowledge of its own nature—and second, his highly intellectualized account of what is doing the driving—not a personal God or deified Superman, but the Idea, something like a system of Platonic Forms. A theology student in his youth, Hegel knows perfectly well how to present this as a version of the orthodox Christian story (in fact he thinks he is improving on it); and he can preach with the best of them, as you'll quickly discover as you read.

But history, surely, is driven by the actions of human beings? And they have their own human schemes, interests, and motives—one thing they *aren't* trying to do is ensure that the Idea comes to perfect self-knowledge. (How could they be? Most of them have never even heard of it.) Now we meet a famous doctrine: the Cunning of Reason. Without their knowledge, the Idea (or Reason) really is at work, influencing and directing them toward its own ends.

Most of Hegel's audience was familiar with the idea of good defeating evil. This folio from the early-fifteenth-century book of hours *Les très riches heures du duc de Berry* shows God and the archangel Michael defeating Satan and the other rebel angels.

So is there an external force, like the ancient Fates, looking down on us and manipulating our lives? No, Hegel's view is subtler and less superstitious than that. Remember that our minds, in Hegel's grand plan, do embody the Idea, but not yet with any clear consciousness of it. (Think of the way a gene—Hegel much approved of organic metaphors—"contains" the adult organism, but will only show it gradually in the process of growth and development.) Because there is this something within us, active though obscure, we can consciously pursue our own limited and individual ends and purposes while really serving the turn of Reason.

The Idea, now as Spirit or *Geist*, directs the course of history through the will of "world-historical individuals" (the famous people you read about in history books). Their feeling for the requirements of Spirit is a little more advanced than that of their contemporaries, their dissatisfaction with the present state of things slightly sharper and better focused. Hegel describes them (never let anyone tell you he couldn't write!): "They do not find their aims and vocation in the calm and regular system of the present . . . they draw their inspiration from another source, that hidden spirit whose hour is near but which still lies beneath the surface and seeks to break out." These are the leaders

Hegel did not believe that human life was controlled by an external force such as the three Fates (the three goddesses who in classical mythology determine the course of human life). The three Fates are shown here with Death in an eighteenth-century rendering by artist Araldo de Luca.

who change the world, unite nations, create empires, found political institutions. And once the new state of things exists, the society or nation comes face-to-face with something it has itself produced—the situation that advances self-understanding, remember—and finds out a little more about its own real aspirations.

It also finds out more about the problems they bring with them. For a start, these transitions from one state to another rarely happen smoothly, without conflict and struggle. What Hegel calls "the calm and regular system of the present" always has its appeal, especially for those in whom the subliminal awareness of Spirit's next move is undeveloped. These become the reactionaries who resist the world-historical individual's striving for change; they are opposed by those of a slightly more advanced state of consciousness, who gather behind the leader, sensing that the new direction is the right one.

Only right *for now*, however. Remember that the strange thing from which we began, the Idea, involves development, in a figurative sense. Everything that exists or happens reflects the Idea, and that of course includes history, which exhibits the Idea's "development," but now in a literal sense. The Idea, as you will find if you ever read Hegel's *Logic* (but be warned, it is desperately hard work), always develops through the conflict of opposed concepts followed by their resolution, which itself turns out to harbor another opposition, upon which a further resolution follows, and so on until the entire system is complete. So it is, therefore, in the political sphere. Conflict issues in a new order, but before too long the new order itself is showing strains; the seeds of the next conflict were already present in it, and once they mature it is swept away in its turn. You may find the metaphysics with which Hegel underpins all this extravagant, wild, and woolly, but when he applies it to human history the result certainly isn't stupid. It is this idea of progress

Brutus and the Ghost of Caesar (1802) by Edward Scriven (1775–1841) shows the ghost of Caesar haunting Marcus Junius Brutus, the leader of a group of senators who assassinated the Roman military and political leader.

arising out of conflict which is known as "dialectic." It pervades the thought of Hegel, but equally that of Marx, which is why Marx's philosophy is often called "dialectical materialism" (see Chapters 6 and 8).

Notice that there is very little comfort here for the individual. The Idea is to come to self-knowledge, and this it must do in human minds, which are the only vehicle around, but no particular human mind is of any concern to it whatever. History throws individuals away once they have served their turn. That is even, or especially, true of world-historical individuals: "their end attained they fall aside like empty husks." Julius Caesar did his bit—and was assassinated.

Napoleon did his—then was defeated, captured, and sent to rot on Elba. An individual is no more than a dispensable instrument. God, supposedly, loves each one of us, but the Idea couldn't care less, so long as there are some of us, and they are doing its business. So it is hard to see Hegelianism becoming a popular mass philosophy, for all its huge influence.

Charles Darwin: *The Origin of Species*

The first thing we can learn from this fascinating book is not to bother too much about drawing a neat sharp line between philosophy and science. The point is not that the line isn't sharp, although I believe that to be true. The point is that the line (if it exists) is not of much importance for philosophy. On any reasonable way of drawing it Darwin's *Origin* is science, more specifically biology. But because of its subject matter, and the claims it makes, very few books have had greater philosophical impact. For it implies a startling thesis about us and how we have come to be as we are. It may not startle us today, but it startled most of his contemporaries to the point of shock; and there are still a number of people trying to perform the difficult balancing act of rejecting it without appearing merely ignorant and prejudiced.

British naturalist Charles Darwin (1809–1882), shown here in an undated photograph, published *On the Origin of Species* in 1859.

In one sense *The Origin of Species* does much more than "imply" the startling thesis: it builds a very carefully constructed case for it, backed by

ON

THE ORIGIN OF SPECIES

BY MEANS OF NATURAL SELECTION,

OR THE

PRESERVATION OF FAVOURED RACES IN THE STRUGGLE
FOR LIFE.

By CHARLES DARWIN, M.A.,

FELLOW OF THE ROYAL, GEOLOGICAL, LINNÆAN, ETC., SOCIETIES;
AUTHOR OF "JOURNAL OF RESEARCHES DURING H. M. S. BEAGLE'S VOYAGE
ROUND THE WORLD."

LONDON:
JOHN MURRAY, ALBEMARLE STREET.
1859.

The right of Translation is reserved.

Although it is accepted as commonplace nowadays that Darwin was referring to humankind in his discussion of natural selection, humanity is barely mentioned in *On the Origin of Species*, whose first-edition title page is shown here.

a wealth of thoughtfully assessed evidence. Darwin was not the first person to propose the theory of natural selection (he tells you a little of the history of the idea in his own introduction to the book), but he was the first to assemble so much evidence for it and so honestly to confront the difficulties it faces. If prior to 1859 you wanted to reject the view that species were mutable, and developed out of other species, and that our own species was no exception, it was easy: just say no. It conflicted with your other (deeply held) beliefs, many experts opposed it, and there existed no serious and plausible statement of the case for it. After 1859 it wasn't easy at all—though of course there were plenty of people who didn't notice.

In another sense, however, "imply" is exactly the right word: Darwin gave no prominence (in this book) to his opinion that just as much as any other species humanity falls under the general theory. Readers who reach the last chapter—or jump to it—will there find, discreetly placed and well apart, two or three unmistakable sentences. Otherwise, silence. A common mistake is to call the book *Origin of the Species*, presumably supposing that we are the species in question. Absolutely not: There is almost nothing about us.

Plenty about pigeons, in fact half of chapter 1. They lend themselves perfectly to Darwin's strategy: start from a case in which it is totally uncontroversial that a breed can be altered by selection—the breeder's selection of which birds to allow to mate with which. (Unsurprisingly, there's also a lot about cattle and sheep and racehorses; prize dahlias get a mention too.) But that doesn't take Darwin quite as far as he wants to go, because it is perfectly possible to reply that human breeders can make only quite slight changes, so that all the strikingly different breeds of pigeon, though modified by human practice, must in the first place have come each from birds of its own particular species—they are just too different to have descended all of them from one type of bird. Surely?

Now Darwin's judgment is at its best. He doesn't try to *prove* his point, but just shows that anyone opposing it will have a lot more talking to do. If there was an original fantail pigeon, where is it now found in the wild? Well, perhaps it has become extinct, or lives somewhere frightfully remote. And how about the other distinctive breeds that pigeon fanciers are interested in—where are their wild relatives? And what of the fact that within these breeds one occasionally finds individuals that closely match the complex coloring of a type of pigeon that *does* exist in the wild nowadays? So is it that all today's distinctive breeds had ancestors of the same coloring (although they were distinct species), and are now all either extinct in the wild or at least have never been observed? Well, well, how very surprising . . .

Drawing of a stock pigeon in *Svenska fåglar, efter naturen och på sten ritade* (1828–1838), by Magnus, Wilhelm, and Ferdinand von Wright.

Another variation on a theme much favored by Victorian cartoonists. Darwin's message wasn't to be digested quickly. This caricature from around 1871, published in *La petite lune*, shows Darwin as a monkey hanging from the Tree of Science.

So if it is probable that artificial selection can produce such effects in a relatively short time, is there any natural principle of selection that might produce effects of similar magnitude, and perhaps of far greater magnitude, given an enormously longer time to work in? Yes, because the "struggle for existence" (about which Darwin writes a very interesting chapter) eliminates many individuals before they are able to reproduce. A fantail pigeon will probably mate only if it catches the eye of the breeder; a wild pigeon will not mate unless it withstands the struggle for existence long enough to reach maturity. What is being selected for is in the two cases utterly different. In the second case it is the capacity to withstand the local environmental/ecological conditions, and if these should become harsh the selection process will be brutally efficient.

Once thoughts like these have brought us to see that very substantial change is possible, indeed positively likely, and when we recall (what was only just becoming clear to geologists when Darwin was a young man) that these processes may have been going on for an almost unthinkable length of time, certain observations strike one differently, like those Darwin offers in one of the very few sentences in which human beings figure: "The framework of bones being the same in the hand of a man, wing of a bat, fin of the porpoise, and leg of the horse—the same number of vertebrae forming the neck of the giraffe and of the elephant . . . at once explain themselves on the theory of descent with slow and slight successive modifications.'

The nineteenth-century enthusiasm for progress, to which the philosophy of Hegel gave such momentum, predisposed many to understand Darwin as part of the same progressivist movement. His younger contemporary Herbert Spencer (1820–1903), a man of a much more metaphysical, even somewhat Hegelian turn of mind, really was part of it. He was the inventor of the overworked phrase "the survival of the fittest," which can easily be understood as implying that those who survive in the struggle for existence are superior to those who do not. He himself seems to have taken it like that, for in the name of progress he opposed anything that would lessen the intensity of the struggle, like social welfare arrangements.

English philosopher, political theorist, and sociological theorist Herbert Spencer coined the phrase *survival of the fittest* in *Principles of Biology* (1864) and extended the concept beyond natural selection into the realm of social welfare.

This kind of thought soon turned into a movement known as social Darwinism. The name is inappropriate to the point of being slanderous. Darwin never drew such conclusions, nor would he have done, for no such thing follows. In his system the words "the fittest" simply mean: those best fitted to survive (and reproduce) under the conditions then obtaining. They have nothing to do with moral, or intellectual, or aesthetic superiority; and they mean nothing at all without the rider "under the conditions then obtaining." If those conditions change, yesterday's "fittest" may be tomorrow's no-hopers. One of the many

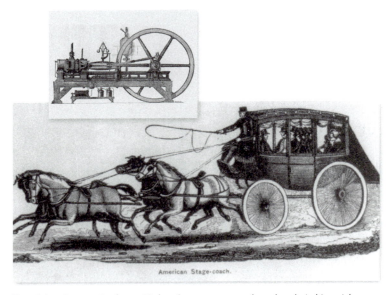

American Stage-coach.

Darwinism does not imply—as Herbert Spencer appears to have thought in his social applications of it—that the forms that survive are superior to those that do not, only that they were better *at surviving and reproducing in the circumstances then obtaining*. No other kind of superiority is implied. And if the circumstances change, superiority may change too. Is the combustion engine (illustration from Dugald Clerk's *The Gas and Oil Engine*, 1896) superior to the horse and cart (engraving from Abby Sage Richardson, *The History of Our Country*, 1875)? Possibly, in some ways—until the world runs out of oil.

problems about making social application of natural selection like Spencer is that changes in human society can so easily produce changes in the conditions under which they themselves arose. Is the internal combustion engine "fitter" than the horse and cart? In a sense, yes, but only so long as it doesn't run the world out of oil.

That doesn't mean that Darwin shouldn't be allowed to change anyone's attitudes to anything—far from it. Here is an example. The literary critic and popularist Christian theologian C. S. Lewis once (though I'm sure not only once) found himself lamenting our sexual drives. Given the opportunity, he wrote, most of us would eat too much, but not enormously too much; whereas if a young man indulged his sexual appetite every time he felt like it, and each act led to a baby, he would in a very short time populate an entire village. Which shows, Lewis concluded, just how perverted our natural sexuality has become.

British writer C. S. Lewis lamented that humanity's natural sexuality had become perverted, but nature is not perverted; it simply runs as it must and does not follow humankind's moral code.

But before you castigate yourself a sinner and start bewailing the lost innocence of the human male, reflect on the lesson of Darwin: what we see here is no perversion of nature; it is simply nature herself, who is not concerned to construct the world in accordance with our moral code or anyone else's. Few factors will, on average, have as big an effect on the numbers of a man's children as the strength and frequency of his sexual urges; so if this is itself something which many of his children inherit from him, it is clearly a characteristic which natural selection will select and enhance. If most of today's males possess it that is just what we should expect, and certainly no call to start speaking of the Fall of Man, perversion, and moral deterioration. Or perhaps what some call original sin is really the fact that what evolution has produced—and was bound to produce—is out of line with their own conception of an ideal human character.

Incidentally: don't worry about all those villages, each populated by several hundred half brothers and sisters. They will only spring up where life provides our young Casanova with a veritable production-line supply of females, willing, fertile, not already pregnant, and not associated with any other males sufficiently aggressive to send him packing. Nature can be relied upon to ensure that this does not happen very often, to put it mildly. C. S. Lewis's imagination was floating well clear of the facts.

That example is specific and relatively trivial, but you can easily see how Darwinism could subvert an entire philosophy, such as one of those we have just seen. For Descartes human reason was a faculty given to us and guaranteed by God, no less, and that was why he could rely on it to tell us about the essential nature of mind and matter, and a good deal else besides. What if instead he had thought of it as a natural instrument which had developed because, *and to the extent that*, it gave its possessors a competitive advantage over those without it? Would he then have supposed that what it appeared to tell us on such matters could with complete confidence be taken to be the truth? If so, how would he have justified it? It is one thing to think that *God* could not be a deceiver, but quite another to say that since the faculty of reason gives us such advantage in practical matters it cannot possibly lead us hopelessly astray when applied to a question like whether the mind is an independent substance. Am I to believe that because reason is good at helping us survive it must also be good at metaphysics? Why on earth should that be true? If Descartes had lived after Darwin (please forgive the historical absurdity) the foundations of his philosophy would have had to be very different, and if they were so different, could the superstructure have been the same?

Nietzsche: *The Genealogy of Morals*

"A philosopher is a terrible explosive from which nothing is safe"— that is the only comment we have heard so far (Chapter 1) from the German philosopher Friedrich Nietzsche (1844–1900). He had no intention of offering his readers a comfortable experience, and his contemporaries defended themselves by just not reading him. But soon after his death the tide began to turn, and he became a major influence on twentieth-century thought, especially on the European continent.

The Genealogy of Morals, first published in 1887, consists of a preface and three essays, all conveniently divided into numbered sections. *Don't* skip the preface. And don't miss the first sentence: "how much we know nowadays, but how little we know about ourselves." A huge change in European thought is under way. The tendency had long been to suppose that, however bewildering and opaque the rest of reality may be to us, at least we could tell what was going on in our own minds; but in the nineteenth century that tendency is fast losing momentum. We have just seen a hint of it in Hegel's understanding of history: the forces of *Geist* are at work in us, though we know nothing or little of it (see above). Less than a generation after Nietzsche came Sigmund Freud (1856–1939), founder of psychoanalysis, with his doctrine of the unconscious mind in which the

In *The Genealogy of Morals,* German philosopher Friedrich Nietzsche, shown here in a photograph taken by F. Hartmann in Basel around 1875, questioned the provenance and the true nature of Christian moral values.

most important causes of our mental lives lie hidden from us. Acquiring self-knowledge is no longer a matter of a quick introspective glance. It calls for hard and painful work, and there is no guarantee that you will like what you find.

Don't miss §3 of the preface either. Do you hear something familiar about it? It reminds me of Part 1 of Descartes's *Discourse on the Method*: still a teenager, the future philosopher is struck by skepticism and mistrust toward the intellectual diet that his seniors are feeding him (see above). For Descartes it had been the neo-Aristotelianism of the universities. For Nietzsche it was the moral values of nineteenth-century Christianity. Were they as self-evident as everyone around him seemed to think? Descartes wanted to inquire into the truth of these "truths" that he was being taught. Nietzsche reckoned it was time for some questions about the value of these "values." His method was to ask about their history, their pedigree, what he called their "genealogy." Where had they come from, how had people come to hold them? Why had they come to hold them, or in other words: what were these values doing for the people whose values they became?

A frequent reaction at this point is to say that the value of something, what it is worth, depends on what it is like *now*. How it came to be that way is quite another matter. So Nietzsche is asking the wrong question. However well he answers it, it won't tell us anything about the value of our values. To think that it will is to commit (some more philosophers' jargon for your growing collection!) the "genealogical fallacy."

But is that criticism altogether fair? I don't think so. There are certainly cases in which our view of what something is worth is very much bound up with our beliefs about how it began, and if those beliefs change, our evaluation of the thing itself is threatened as well. Indeed we have just seen a very important example, one which was important for Nietzsche too: the effect of Darwinism on our conception of ourselves. For so many of Darwin's contemporaries the human race originated in a decision by God to create us in his own image. The idea that we had in fact developed from inferior things like monkeys by a distinctly chancy process that might just as easily not have happened wasn't just a new fact to take on board, like the existence of one more previously undiscovered planet; it was a slap in the face for human dignity and their conception of their own worth—which was why it was doggedly resisted then and is resisted by some to this day. No doubt about it: under the right circumstances, genealogies can be just as explosive as Nietzsche intended—so back to the question about moral values.

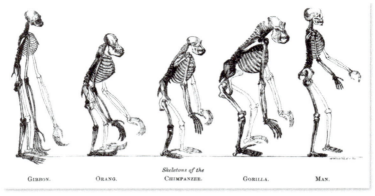

Skeletons of the
GIBBON.   ORANG.   CHIMPANZEE.   GORILLA.   MAN.

The idea that humanity had developed from inferior animals instead of being created by God in his own image was felt by many to be a slap in the face to human dignity. The frontispiece to English biologist Thomas Henry Huxley's *Evidence as to Man's Place in Nature* (1863), comparing the skeletons of various apes to that of man, illustrates the evolutionary line of thought, whereas the illustration from the 1702 edition of Altus's *Mutus liber* (Mute book) (first published in 1677), depicting a cosmological scene showing concentric circles portraying Creation, illustrates the creationist point of view.

Many believed, and some still do, that moral values were of similar origin: handed down to human beings direct from God. Nietzsche, who in spite of his clerical home background once described himself as an atheist by instinct, had no interest whatever in that story; he sought the origin of human values in human needs and human psychology. (*Human, All Too Human* is the pregnant title of one of his earlier books.)

He wasn't the first to do so, as becomes clear in preface §4. In fact, there was already a tradition of it, and Nietzsche took its central thesis, broadly stated, to be something along the following lines: when humans found certain types of behavior (on the part of individuals) advantageous to them and the smooth running of their society, they called them "good," and strongly encouraged them; where they found them disadvantageous, the reverse. That, simply, is how behaving for the good of others rather than one's own came to be regarded as good—the others declared it to be good, because of the benefit they received.

On the face of it that sounds quite plausible: a society reinforces what is beneficial to it. But Nietzsche regarded it as sentimental, unhistorical claptrap. Drawing on his expert knowledge of ancient languages (he had had, and then abandoned, a meteoric academic career) he told a very different tale. Far from its being those who received benefits from the behavior of others who then called those others (and their behavior) "good," it was the upper classes, the aristocracy, the nobility, the rulers of ancient societies who first called themselves (and their way of life) good and the ordinary people, the slaves, the subject population, bad. Early good/bad distinctions are perhaps better understood as distinctions between "noble" and "base," free and enslaved, leaders and led, the washed and the unwashed. They were the words in which the top dogs celebrated themselves, their strength, and their own way of life, and expressed the extent of the gap that they felt between themselves and the weak, impoverished, servile masses.

That's also pretty plausible—you can just imagine them thinking and talking that way. (You can still hear it going on nowadays if you get into the right company.) But it was the next step which, according to Nietzsche, was the decisive one for the next two thousand years and more of European morality: the worm turned, the masses revolted. He isn't talking about violent revolution, armed struggle, for which the underclasses were generally too weak, both materially and spiritually, but about something much subtler and much more insidious. They relieved their frustration and resentment in one of the very few ways that were open to them, namely, by developing their own system of values in which everything about their oppressors was "bad" and they themselves, whose lives contrasted with theirs in so many ways, were "good."

So this value system was not God-given, and it was not the outcome of some intuitive perception of its truth, or intrinsic "rightness." It was a vengeful, retaliatory device, born of the weak's resentment of the strong. All that commitment to charity, compassion, and love was actually fueled by *hate*. This kind of thought is entirely typical of Nietzsche, who loved to stand popular conceptions on their head. Just when you thought your house was in good order, along comes a Nietzschean "explosion" and suddenly your roof has changed places with your cellar. This is philosophy at its most challenging. Natural iconoclasts will just love it, but anyone can admire the fireworks.

Just these facts (as he believed) about the origins of the morality of love and compassion wouldn't have made Nietzsche so profoundly mistrustful of it as he actually was. After all, in adopting and promoting it the masses were trying, in the only way open to them, to gain power

Nietzsche sought the source of human values in human needs and human psychology, and he was not alone in his quest. A strong tradition had already developed that said that humans found certain types of behavior beneficial to them and labeled them good, and that this was how behaving for the good of others rather than one's own came to be considered good—others declared it to be so because of the benefits they received. Nietzsche disagreed, however, declaring that it was the members of the upper class who had first called the ordinary people bad and *themselves* good; they hadn't come to the aid of the ordinary people and been designated good by them as tradition had supposed. In this print published in the December 18, 1869, issue of *Harper's Weekly*, African American slaves use a cotton gin while their masters check the results of their work.

over the strong, and he has nothing against that—all life, in his view, is a manifestation of the will to power, and no tiny little human moralist has any business pronouncing on life in general. What he most dislikes about "herd morality" is that it arose not through *affirmation* of their own way of life (like the codes of the higher classes) but through the *negation* of someone else's: they looked at the vigorous, free, proud, self-assured, self-assertive people who ruled them, resentfully declared their qualities to be bad and hence the opposite qualities, such as passivity, servitude, humility, unselfishness, to be good. Herd morality is life denying, in Nietzsche's estimation.

Those who espoused this morality were now in a very strained position. As living beings they embodied the same instinctive will to power as did the ruling class, but unlike them they had no natural outlet for it. So when their instincts led them to seek a different kind of power by pronouncing their masters' masterful instincts to be vices they were in fact turning against their own instincts as well. So, to add to the fact that they were needy and oppressed, these people were psychologically sick, inwardly divided. And they felt pretty wretched.

But help—of a sort—is at hand, in the form of a figure known to every culture and epoch and of intense interest to Nietzsche: the ascetic priest, committed to poverty, humility, and chastity, and in some cases practicing quite extreme forms of self-torture. This figure, who represents at its most explicit the wish to be rid of the bodily conditions of life and to escape into something otherworldly and "beyond," denies life more emphatically than anyone else. So, like the herd, he is sick, but much stronger than they are—a strength which manifests itself in his ability to adopt and sustain his way of life.

This strength gives him power, the power to lead and direct the flock of weaker souls. It arises partly from their perception of his inward strength, partly from the air of mystery and esoteric knowledge

For Nietzsche, the ascetic priest provided the suffering flock with a reason for their suffering and an outlet for their resentment of the upper classes. This 1599 engraving by Cherubino Alberti (1552–1615) depicts ascetic St. Francis of Assisi.

with which the ascetic surrounds himself. But it also arises in part from the fact that he does them a service: he alleviates their suffering. Remember that they suffer because they have set themselves against their own vital instincts; so he can hardly be expected to *cure* their suffering, because he too sets himself against his vital instincts, only more openly, with greater determination and singleness of purpose.

An important fact about human suffering is that people will put up with a great deal if only they *understand the reason* for it—even glory in it, if they find the reason good enough. Another is that those who are suffering want to find *someone to blame* for it—that acts as a kind of anesthetic, blocking the pain out with an overlay of anger.

The priest instinctively knows this, and gives his flock both a reason for their suffering and an author of it. They are suffering to make their souls fit for heaven, or for the victory of justice, or for the sake of truth, or so that God's kingdom should come on earth—all fine things to suffer for. Who is to blame for the suffering? Answer: they *themselves*. With this stroke the seething resentment of the masses is directed away from the rulers, its original objects, conflict with whom will most likely only lead them into more suffering, perhaps partial annihilation. Redirected onto themselves it may at least provide strength and motivation for a little self-discipline and self-improvement—under priestly instruction. And they are ready to accept it, for as we saw they have already turned against their own instincts and so in one sense against themselves. They know what has to be rooted out: any hint in themselves of the attitudes and behavior characteristic of the strong. They have been rendered harmless.

Such is Nietzsche's analysis. Whatever else we may think of it, it is certainly unflinching. These are no more than a few of the main thoughts, crudely compressed. Nietzsche's style, its musicality, its energy, its variety, its biting wit, is something one can only experience for oneself. And the text is full of delightful detail, like the account of the real philosopher in §7 of the third essay. Or take the first essay, §§7–9. Do you find this anti-Semitic in tone? Then read it again, and you will see that it is really aimed at anti-Semitism itself. What it says is that it was only the moral history of the Jews which created the psychological climate in which Christianity could arise—Nietzsche is firing an ironic salvo at those Christian anti-Semites who grounded their anti-Semitism on the premise that it was Jews who were responsible for the crucifixion of Christ. Once again he has turned a popular way of thinking upside down: Christians should *revere* Jews, because they have the Jews to thank for the success of Christianity. Delicious stuff!

EIGHT

What's in It for Whom?

●

THINKING ABOUT PHILOSOPHY IS HARD WORK—you may have noticed, though if you've got this far at least it hasn't put you off. Writing the stuff is even harder. (Take it from me.) So why have people done either? Well, for one or more of a whole catalogue of reasons. In the hope of learning to control nature, or of learning to control themselves, to get to heaven, to avoid going to hell; to enable us to bear life as it is, to make life bearable by changing it; to shore up institutions political, moral, or intellectual, or to tear them down; to promote the writer's interests, to promote other people's interests (yes, that happens too), even to promote everybody's interests; because they can't stand certain other philosophers; because their job demands it.

Whether it begins as the desire to control nature, to get to heaven, to make life bearable, to shore up institutions or to tear them down, most philosophy attempts to do something for somebody, and to succeed, that philosophy must have a constituency, a group of interested parties. In this engraving by John Boydell from around 1768, a philosopher gives a lecture to students young and old.

Perhaps just occasionally out of pure curiosity. There is a widespread idea that philosophers are unworldly people, remote from reality. If that refers to their lifestyle, it may frequently have been true, though not always. If it refers to their work, then (I am speaking now of philosophy that *endures*) it is usually false—at least in the sense that they are almost always addressing some real concern and claiming to offer some real improvement.

Right back at the beginning (Chapter 1) I spoke of three big questions: what should I do? what is there? (i.e., what is reality like?) and how do we know? It might sound as if any philosophy offering human beings some real improvement must be concerned primarily with the first of those. But that wouldn't be right. Beliefs about how things are can serve to give a meaning to life or bolster our feelings of self-worth, as, for example, the belief that we are made in the image of God; they can give a rationale to (or serve as an excuse for) certain types of behavior, like the belief that humans have rational souls and animals don't. Answers to the question "how do we know?" can strengthen, or loosen, the hold that various answers to the first two types of question have on us; and very importantly, they can imply beliefs about *who* has knowledge, with obvious consequences for the prestige and power of members of that group.

Most philosophy attempts, then, to do something for somebody. To finish, let's look at some philosophy from this perspective. If it is to endure, a philosophy needs a constituency, a group of interested parties. Its chances are best if the constituency is a large one. First, a couple of philosophies devoted to the individual. That's a big constituency—we're all individuals.

The Individual

The philosophy of Epicurus (see Chapter 5) is addressed to the individual; it offers a recipe, backed by argument, for living a happy life. Social and political arrangements are unjust if they interfere with individuals' attempts to apply the recipe; otherwise, his only political recommendation is not to engage in politics. You can to some degree help others to live the right sort of life, but only those close to you (Epicureanism strongly advocates friendship); everyone must follow the recipe for themselves. For success depends not on material conditions, the sort of thing one person can arrange for another, but on your attitude toward them. And that is precisely the point, since happiness comes of knowing that your state of mind is largely independent of whatever life may tip on you next.

It may then surprise you to hear that in Epicurus's opinion the only good is pleasure. Surely how much pleasure we can get depends heavily on our material conditions of life? But there's a second surprise: he thinks that the highest possible pleasure is freedom from physical pain and mental anxiety. Simple, easily attainable pleasures are no less pleasant than extravagant and exotic ones; and reliance on the latter induces anxiety: the means to obtain them may be taken away from you. (The idea that Epicureanism is a constant dinner party with musicians and dancing girls is completely misleading—it must have come down to us from Epicurus's opponents, who were numerous.)

A cause of much mental turmoil is superstitious fear. Banish it. Realize that in their perfect bliss the gods have neither need nor wish to interfere in human affairs. Learn enough about physics, astronomy, and meteorology to feel confident that all phenomena have natural

Epicureanism in practice? Not according to Epicurus. *The Way You Hear It Is the Way You Sing It (As the Old Sing, So Twitter the Young)* is an oil on canvas by Jan Steen from around 1665.

explanations—they are not portents, omens, or signs of divine wrath. And do not fear death, for death is simply nonexistence, in which there can be nothing to fear. That, on a thumbnail, is Epicurus's advice to each one of us. You could do a lot worse than follow it. Of course there wouldn't be any politicians if we all did; but perhaps we could put up with that.

Epicurus taught the individual to be inwardly armed against whatever may befall. Over two thousand years later John Stuart Mill wrote a stirring defense of every individual's right to shape his or her own life. In his famous essay *On Liberty* (1859) he argued for what has become known as the Harm Principle: "the only purpose for which power can be rightfully exercised over any member of a civilized community . . . is to prevent harm to others." As democratic systems of government became better entrenched in Europe and America they also became better understood, and Mill had spotted a latent danger: the tyranny of the majority over the individual and over minority groups.

As befits the author of *Utilitarianism* (see Chapter 5) he makes no appeal to human rights, but rather to the damage done, the value lost, if his principle is not observed. To be master of one's own life is a good for human beings, a part of our happiness, so the individual loses even if what the law forbids them to do is something they wouldn't have

Nineteenth-century British philosopher John Stuart Mill, shown here in a photograph of a painting by George Frederick Watts from the early twentieth century, was somewhat similar to Epicurus in believing that the one thing valuable in itself was happiness, defined as pleasure and the absence of pain.

done anyway. But the whole society loses too. For the people whom the Harm Principle protects are an extremely valuable resource, precisely because they have unconventional opinions and unusual lifestyles. If their opinions are in fact true the value to the community is obvious. If they are false it is less obvious but equally real: if truth is wholly unopposed it becomes a dead formula on the tongue—opposition ensures that it remains live in the mind. As for unconventional lifestyles, they provide living experimental data from which everyone can learn. Constraining the individual damages everybody.

The State

Earlier (Chapter 2, and again briefly in Chapter 5) we looked at the so-called contract theory of political obligation. We saw it in action in Plato's *Crito*, and noticed that it can in principle take many forms, arising from the variety of possible answers to the question: who contracts with whom to do what on what conditions?

Of all contract theories, that of Thomas Hobbes (1588–1679) is perhaps the most famous—and if so then because of his marvelously unflattering description of the "state of nature," life before any social arrangements had been made, in which nobody can own anything, cultivate anything, or do anything constructive at all without continual fear of being attacked and robbed, with a fair chance of being murdered thrown in. As long as this "war . . . of every man against every man" lasts, life is "solitary, poor, nasty, brutish and short." So how to improve matters? Form an association; agree to accept the authority of a "sovereign" (person or body) with full powers to do anything they deem needful to protect each of you from the others and from any external threat. This sovereign body can do no injustice, since as their accepted representative everything it does is done with the presumed consent of all who are party to the contract that set it up. Only if the sovereign directly threatens their lives may the citizens resist—for it was to protect their lives that they entered into the contract in the first place. The "Laws and Constitution of Athens," you recall (*Crito* 50e–51c, Chapter 2 above), wouldn't allow Socrates even that much, but gave little reason to support such extreme claims.

Mightn't Hobbes's citizens reply that it wasn't just to protect their lives that they entered into the contract? It was to enjoy various liberties, all of which were lacking in the state of nature. That would suggest that

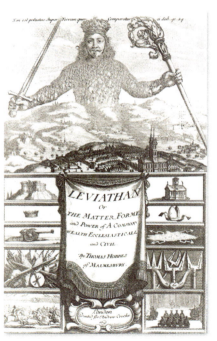

the citizens' right of resistance kicks in rather earlier than the point at which their very lives are threatened. (Besides, having handed over all the power, how are they to protect their lives?) Like Plato, Hobbes seems to have

Thomas Hobbes held that before any social arrangements had been made, or as he says in *The Leviathan*, as long as this "war . . . of every man against every man" lasted, no one could accomplish anything because of the constant threat of attack from other members of the human race. The title page of *The Leviathan*, published in 1651, is shown here.

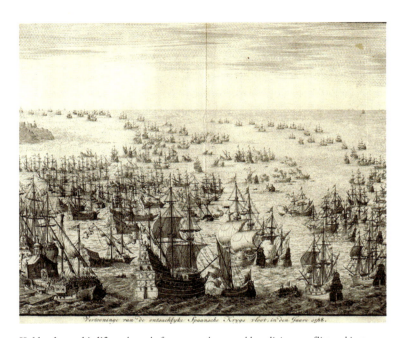

Hobbes began his life at the end of a century devastated by religious conflict and just as the Spanish Armada, shown in a mighty display in a 1679 print by Dutch artist Jan Luyken, approached his homeland, so his philosophy—though he may have gone further than his arguments warrant—is understandable in the light of his circumstances.

gone further than his arguments warrant. But really that isn't surprising. Plato's youth coincided with Athens's disastrous war against Sparta. Hobbes was born as the Spanish Armada approached, toward the end of a century torn by religious conflict that cost millions of lives, and his maturity witnessed England's descent into civil war. No wonder that both men believed that the prime need of political life was government strong enough to maintain peace and order, the values without which no others could even begin. Their way of supporting the individual was

Seventeenth-century English philosopher John Locke, shown in an oil on canvas from 1697 by portrait painter Sir Godfrey Kneller, poked fun at Hobbes's extreme response to the "war of every man against every man." The second of his *Two Treatises of Government* puts forth a social contract theory that counters Hobbes's absolutist approach.

to hand over total sovereignty to the state. No surprise that some have thought that they went too far. John Locke (1632–1704), writing less than fifty years after Hobbes but in somewhat less threatening political circumstances, waxed ironical:

As if when men quitting the state of nature entered into society, they agreed that all of them but one, should be under the restraint of laws, but that he should still retain all the liberty of the state of nature, increased by power, and made licentious by impunity. This is to think that men are so foolish, that they take care to avoid what mischiefs may be done them by pole-cats, or foxes, but are content, nay think it safety, to be devoured by lions.

The Priesthood

Priests are not generally persons of either wealth or military strength. So whatever gives them security, and not just security but often very considerable power within their society or religious group, must be something else. It arises from what their people *think* about them, what they take them to be able to do for them, the value that they put upon them. In other words, it arises from philosophy. The less tangible and immediate the benefits and the dangers, the more powerful the apparatus needed to maintain belief in them and faith in those who confer (or avert) them.

This isn't a matter of intentional deception—though it would be absurd to suggest that no such thing ever occurs. It isn't even a question of whether what the priestly class would have the laity believe about them is true or false. The point is that it should be believed: otherwise, no priests. So plenty of writing exists which promotes their status.

Illustrations exist everywhere, so since we haven't set foot outside Western Europe for the last few chapters let's return to India and look at the opening chapter of one of the major Upanishads. By the time *The Questions of King Milinda* was written, the *Bṛhadāranyaka Upanishad* (*BU*, see the bibliography) may well have been as old as Chaucer's *Canterbury Tales* today. It belongs to the world of the Hindu Vedas, a world of ritual, sacrifices, and chants that are highly beneficial, though only if correctly performed. To ensure correct performance, you need an expert learned in Vedic matters; for a major ritual you even need a superexpert who makes sure that the other experts are performing correctly. Such expertise needs to be accorded due respect, and no doubt a due fee. ("I wish I had wealth so I could perform rites" is said to be everyone's desire [1. 4. 17]). This expertise—and the perks attaching to it—is the (hereditary) privilege of a particular social class or caste, the Brahmins. No mere social convention, this caste system, as 1. 4. 11 tells us—apparently it arises out of the way the gods themselves were created. Read 1. 4. 11 very carefully: notice how it ascribes a certain superiority to the Kṣatriya, the ruling aristocratic warrior class, while maintaining a certain priority for the Brahmins. Their power is "the womb" of the power of the rulers— that from which it issues. So it's a bad idea for a warrior to injure a priest, for he harms the source of his own power. This is philosophy and theology, but clearly it is good practical politics as well.

This photograph from between 1900 and 1923 shows a brahman priest in India painting his forehead with the red and white marks of his sect and caste.

A reader new to this tradition of thought will find much that is strikingly alien. There is the doctrine of the correspondences between the parts of the sacrificial horse (this was the most prestigious of the Vedic sacrifices) and parts or aspects of the world: the year, the sky, the earth. There is the faith in etymology, as when a longer word is shown to be made up—approximately—of two shorter words, and this fact is taken as indicating the genesis or inner nature of whatever it is that the longer word describes. The knowledge of this strange lore, the text repeatedly insists, is highly advantageous: "A man who knows this will stand firm wherever he may go"; and "Whoever knows this, . . . death is unable to seize him . . . and he becomes one of these deities." So we should value this knowledge, and therefore we should value the people who guard it—the priests.

It isn't necessarily what the priest can do *for* you—it may be what he can do *to* you. Don't go messing about with a Brahmin's wife. As *BU* 6. 4. 12 makes abundantly clear, he will know just the ritual for getting back at you. And "a man cursed by a Brahmin having this knowledge is sure to depart from this world bereft of his virility and stripped of his good works. . . . Never try to flirt with the wife of a learned Brahmin who knows this, lest one make an enemy of a man with this knowledge." You have been warned.

Of course it isn't just priests who need to be needed. It's also doctors and garbagemen and game show hosts and advertising consultants. And—I almost forgot—philosophy professors. They all exist because of people's beliefs and values, hopes and fears.

The Working Classes

The industrialization of Western Europe brought wealth to a few and the most deplorable conditions of life to many. The many quickly found a champion in Karl Marx (1818–83), whose work, it is no exaggeration to say, changed the political face of all those parts of the globe where there was such a thing as politics at all. Only in the last decade has its influence begun to wane. It may have been a victim of its own success—after all, there is no test of a theory like actually trying it out. (That's the principle which underlies the enormous power of the experimental method in the sciences.) And no political theory ever gets a proper trial unless a lot of people are already convinced of it.

Here we have an opportunity to spot some of those connections which are to be found all over the history of philosophy. Marx was no disciple of Hegel—in some respects he was violently opposed to him. But nobody of that time was untouched by Hegelianism. Like Hegel, Marx held that history exhibits a necessary progression; unlike Hegel, he held the driving force to be economic: the material conditions of life. Like Hegel, he held that progress was essentially the resolution of conflict; but the conflict was between the economic interests of different sections of society—hence the famous "class struggle" of the Marxists. And he held a version of the doctrine we saw to be so important to Hegel: the value of being in touch with your "Other," something that "has something of yourself in it," as we often say.

Marx made full use of this idea in his analysis of the contemporary economic system, characterized by the conflict of interest between the working classes and the capitalists, the owners of the "means of production" (i.e., the factories). His sympathies lay firmly with the current underdogs, the workers. The crucial thing was that they, needing to make a living and having nothing else to sell, were selling their labor—working in return for a wage. Not much of a wage, because those buying their labor had no interest in paying them any more than was necessary to keep them working. This ensured for them and their families a life of acute and degrading poverty.

Karl Marx was the founder of communism, and his sympathies lay solidly with the working class. Nearly half a century after his death, Marx's battle to uplift the workers and strike down capitalism was still being fought, as workers were exhorted in this election poster, which shows a man fighting a serpent representing capitalism, to "Vote Communist."

But another, more spiritual, feature of the situation was pressing heavily on them too—the fact that the work they were doing was not really *their* work: "the work is external to the worker, it is not a part of his nature . . . not the satisfaction of a need, merely a means to satisfying other needs. . . . in work he does not belong to himself but to someone else." The unsatisfied need is the need to express *oneself* in what one does.

Diagnosis is one thing; a cure is another. It turns out to be just as possible to experience alienation when the work one is doing is not one's own but the state's as when it is not one's own but the company's.

This undated photo shows men and women on an assembly line putting face cream into jars at a Chicago factory.

That much identification with the interests of the community, when the community is a large and complex one, is not easily achieved or maintained. And even if it were, that would just help to make work *endurable*. If what you do is stand by a conveyor belt tightening the lids on jars of marmalade it may make things less intolerable to be doing it for Mother Russia than for the Global Marmalade Corporation. But that does nothing whatever to make it something positive, an expression of your personality or skills or a means to the development of your potential. Nowadays we speak of "job satisfaction." Not all of us get it—the problem hasn't gone away.

Women

We have been bounding from topic to topic, person to person, across the globe and three millennia like a package tour gone mad. But nobody has been introduced to philosophy until they have seen, in at least one case, a little more deeply into some one philosopher's mind. We have had a glimpse of two famous works by John Stuart Mill, *Utilitarianism* and *On Liberty*. The first told us that the Good was happiness, the second that happiness requires individual freedom. His almost equally famous essay *The Subjection of Women* (1869) tells us that that means everyone, not just adult males.

The practical politician in Mill takes aim at a quite specific and (in theory at least) easily remedied abuse: "the legal subordination of one sex to the other is wrong in itself, and now one of the chief hindrances to human improvement; . . . it ought to be replaced by a principle of perfect equality." Present family law, he argued, amounted to the enslavement of wives. He meant the word quite literally, as his account of the legal position in Chapter 2 shows. What he wants changed,

MILL'S LOGIC, OR FRANCHISE FOR FEMALES
" Pray clear the way, there, for these—ah—persons."

In his essay *The Subjection of Women* (1869), English philosopher John Stuart Mill espoused the rights of women, including their right to vote. This contemporary cartoon shows Mill with suffragettes.

however, is the entire package of practices and opinions which deny women equal educational opportunities and then equal access, on merit, to all occupations and positions of influence.

Any major philosophy needs potential beneficiaries, even in cases where the benefit may be imaginary. In seeking to improve the lot of women Mill has plenty of beneficiaries to appeal to. But he believes that the constituency for his views is 100 percent of mankind, not just 50. He writes about the injustice to women and the damage done to their lives by existing conditions, but he writes almost as much about the loss to everybody. The suppression of women's talents is "a tyranny to them and a detriment to society." History tells us a good deal about what women can do, because women have done it. It tells us nothing about what they can't do, and it never will until they are routinely given the opportunity. (As I write, 130-something years later, a young woman is in the lead in the closing stages of a single-handed around-the-world sailing race, an event that must make demands on mental and physical stamina beyond anything I can imagine.)

Mill also believes that men are damaged as individuals, often in ways they are not likely to notice (which is itself part of the damage). For it is not good for anyone to be brought up to believe themselves superior to others, especially when it happens, as it frequently does, to be others whose faculties are in fact superior to theirs. On the other hand, harsh though it may sound, living one's life around a close relationship with someone of inferior "ability and cultivation" is detrimental to the superior party. Yet many men find themselves in just this situation, married to women whose limitations are no less real just because they are an enforced artificial product of a thoroughly pernicious system. Those men may think they are winning, but the truth is that everyone's a loser.

Thank goodness things have improved since 1869. A bit. In some parts of the world. For the time being.

Given our topic it would be strange to draw attention only to something written by a man. But there is an obvious, indeed almost obligatory, place to turn. Simone de Beauvoir's massive *The Second Sex* (1949) has been the inspiration of so much feminist writing ever since. Were I allowed a brief return to life in about two hundred years' time I would not be surprised to find it rated one of the most influential books of the twentieth century.

The French writer Simone de Beauvoir is shown here in a photograph taken in 1946 or 1947, two or three years before the publication of her highly influential *The Second Sex*.

Like Mill, Beauvoir is concerned with the liberty of women; unlike Mill, she is not particularly concerned with the connection between liberty and happiness. She denies that there are any interesting general statements about what women are like, for what they are like is a response to their circumstances, some of which are social and therefore highly variable. (Mill appeared to think that there might be some such generalizations, but denied that any were known.) Besides, Beauvoir stands in the existentialist tradition and holds that how we react to our circumstances is a free decision for each of us—to pretend that we are wholly determined by our circumstances is *inauthenticity*, abdication of responsibility.

I have space enough only to touch one of the themes of this long and constantly lively book. In Chapter 7 I spoke of the enormous influence of Hegel, and mentioned his doctrine of self-knowledge: it arises when one meets aspects of oneself in something else, or one's "Other." Seizing on the psychological truth in this, while completely ignoring Hegel's grand metaphysics, Beauvoir develops her most characteristic doctrine: woman is man's Other, and the self-understanding of both depends on it.

When the Other is itself a subject, a person, the situation becomes more complicated and potentially very damaging. I'm watching you watching me watching you . . . How A sees B affects B, so it alters what A finds in B. And this (recall the doctrine about self-knowledge) alters A's perception of A, which then affects A, both of which affect how A sees B . . . Just once get something badly wrong, as when man enslaved woman, thinking that that was good for him, and woman accepted enslavement, thinking that was the only choice for her, and all relations between the sexes are going to get entangled in a net of error and artificiality. Now "whatever he does . . . he feels tricked and she feels wronged." The reciprocity of the relationship means that neither party alone can put it right: Beauvoir appeals simultaneously to men to recognize the independence and equality of women, and to women to become just that, by realizing that it is indeed the truth about themselves.

So on the very last page comes a sentence which, while completely characteristic of Beauvoir, could almost have been written by Mill: "when we abolish the slavery of half of humanity, together with the whole system of hypocrisy that it implies, then the 'division' of humanity will reveal its genuine significance and the human couple will find its true form." He, coming from the empiricist and utilitarianism tradition, and she, against the totally different background of Hegel plus existentialism, end up remarkably close together. It almost makes you think they might be right . . .

Animals

Anyone promoting the interests of animals—nonhuman animals—faces an initial problem: animals can't read. So the writer will have to convince an audience distinct from the group he seeks to benefit, which calls for one or both of two strategies: either appeal to their better nature, or argue that they will benefit too. We saw the second of those at work in attempts to engage the support of the laity for the priesthood; Mill and Beauvoir used both in trying to rally men to the cause of women's emancipation.

The situation is even less promising when most of those to whom you are appealing benefit, or think they benefit, from the very practices you are trying to have abolished. Lots of people like to eat meat; lots of people believe that humans benefit enormously from medical

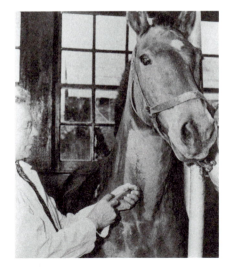

This photograph from around 1944 shows a biologist injecting a horse with diphtheria bacteria at the New York City Department of Health serum and vaccine farm in Otisville, New York.

Two sacred cows wander through the streets of Hyderabad, India.

research conducted by means of experiments on animals. Feminist writers had something of the same problem when they tried to win men over to their views, but at least they had a direct constituency in women; "animalists" have no direct constituency at all.

Buddhism, without going to extremes, is naturally protective toward animals. I say "naturally," because Buddhism retains the Hindu belief that souls return again and again to life, and that what is in one incarnation a human may in another be an animal. The Buddha once lived as a hare. Christianity had no such metaphysics, nor the attached scruples—ask an Indian cow whether metaphysics matters! Adam was created lord over the animals, and they were created for the use of mankind. We have rational souls, but they don't, which leaves them outside the moral sphere. (St. Thomas Aquinas [1225–74] said so, among others.) That one ran and ran. Hume took a pop at it (see Chapter 3), but still it went on running.

As the founder of the utilitarianism that Mill espoused and developed, Jeremy Bentham (1748–1832) took pain and pleasure to be the morally decisive categories, and famously declared of animals: "The question is not, Can they reason? nor, Can they talk? but, Can they suffer?" (They can, of course, so they enter into the utilitarian equation and we have moral responsibilities toward them.) But that was an incidental passage from a book devoted to human welfare. It was only very recently that we began to get whole books explicitly about the morality of our treatment of animals (see the bibliography), a fact which may reflect the tricky tactical situation which their authors have to address.

Their doctrines have made enormous progress over the last twenty or thirty years—the tactical problem wasn't insoluble. They were able to appeal to the sentimentality of those who like to ascribe human characteristics to animals. They were able to appeal to the much harder facts of modern biology, which show, far more convincingly than Hume could have done, that our relationship to animals is a lot closer than Aquinas ever imagined. They appealed powerfully to people's consciences, asking Bentham's question whether the suffering of animals could be justified by resulting good for humans, and if so, then when? For you might feel a difference between the death of experimental mice in return for a substantial advance in the treatment of cancer, and the death of dogs and bears in a bear pit for the sake of a few minutes of sport.

Some aspects of animal welfare tie in with another pressing concern—the whole business of damage to, and care for, the natural environment. One such aspect, vegetarianism, is sometimes treated in that way. Using vegetable materials to feed cattle, and then eating the meat, is said to be a very inefficient way of using the Earth's resources, compared with eating the vegetables straight off and cutting out the cow in between. So vegetarianism is presented as being, long-term, in everyone's self-interest. Good move—the more people are listening, the more point in talking.

Professional Philosophers

You will have noticed, perhaps with some surprise, that I have said nothing about philosophy as it is being written now. That some of it is of value, and will last, I have little doubt, and even less doubt that what lasts will be a tiny fraction of what is now being published. I could guess at one or two titles, but a guess is exactly what it would be; so I have preferred to stick to work which we already know to have survived a substantial test of time. Part of the reason why it has survived the test is that it was written out of a real feeling that its message was needed for the benefit of humanity, and we can recognize the passion in it as well as the intelligence.

There is no reason why today's philosophical writing shouldn't be like this, and some of it is. But one should be aware that most of it is written by professionals, people whose livelihood and career prospects require them to write and publish on philosophy. Nothing *follows* from that—after all, Kant and Hegel were professional philosophers too. And it certainly doesn't follow that their interest in philosophy isn't genuine. But it does mean that among the various reasons for them to be interested, some are what I might call artificial. Back in Chapter 1 I spoke of philosophers as entering debate to change the course of civilization, not to solve little puzzles. But in today's world of professionalized philosophy the most brilliant solution of a puzzle can get its author a very long way indeed; the temptations and pressures are there to write on puzzles, for other professional philosophers, and let civilization take its own course.

A professional philosopher—be just a little wary of this man.

That is not—please!—to be read as a blanket condemnation of everything now emerging from university philosophy departments. It is meant as advice to someone making their first approach to philosophy with the help of this short introduction. If you are leafing through the latest philosophy book from some academic press, or a recent issue of a top professional journal, and find yourself unable to see what is going on or what claim it could possibly have on your attention, don't transfer your reaction to the whole of philosophy en bloc. It may be that you are looking at a detail from some much larger picture that you don't yet have the experience to recognize. Or the worst may be true, and you really are reading the philosopher's equivalent of a chess problem, something highly ingenious but with no wider significance. While developing your own powers of discrimination, stick to the good old classics.

For no such doubts need arise about any of the philosophers I have tried to introduce you to. We know that they were writing from the heart as well as from the head. Alongside their enormous merits they may have their faults, to be sure: unsuspected ignorance, prejudice, overconfidence, obscurity—just to get the list started. But as I hope to have indicated, philosophy is as wide as life, and in its huge literature are exemplified most intellectual vices as well as most intellectual virtues. Wishing it were otherwise would be close to wishing that human beings didn't have minds.

BIBLIOGRAPHY
WHERE TO GO NEXT?

•

My time is up. But I promised to leave you with the names and addresses, so to speak, of some guides with whom you can begin to go further and deeper. It is worth noticing that some very prominent philosophers have devoted time and care to writing introductions. This is no matter of churning out a standard textbook: every route into philosophy is to some extent personal.

INTRODUCTIONS

T. Nagel, *What Does It All Mean?* (New York: Oxford University Press, 1987).

In this very short book Tom Nagel, eschewing all mention of history and aiming straight for the problems, gives the reader a taste of nine different areas: knowledge, other people's minds, the mind-body relation, language and meaning, freedom of the will, right and wrong, justice, death, and the meaning of life. Just right for your first piece of reading—see what grabs you.

S. W. Blackburn, *Think* (Oxford: Oxford University Press, 1999).

The perfect thing to move on to after Nagel. Takes on several of the same themes as Nagel's book, plus God and Reasoning, now at greater length and depth; frequent quotation of historical sources, so beginning to communicate a sense of the (Western) philosophical tradition. Very entertainingly written.

B. Russell, *The Problems of Philosophy* (Oxford: Oxford University Press, 1912).

A classic introductory book, still going after nearly ninety years. Don't miss the last chapter—Russell's claims for the value of philosophy—even though some of it may nowadays seem just a little grandiose and optimistic.

HISTORIES OF PHILOSOPHY

B. Russell, *History of Western Philosophy* (London: George Allen and Unwin, 1946).

A remarkable book synthesizing a mountain of material in a most engaging way. Enjoy it, but don't be surprised if you later hear the opinion that Russell's account of some particular thinker is limited, or misses the main point, or is distorted by his intense dislike of Christianity.

F. Copleston, *A History of Philosophy*, 8 vols. (London: Burns and Oates, 1946–66).

Nothing like so much fun as Russell, but comprehensive and reliable and suitable for serious study. With a different publisher (Search Press), Copleston later added a volume on French philosophy from the Revolution onward, and another on philosophy in Russia.

S. Radhakrishnan, *Indian Philosophy*, 2 vols. (Delhi: Oxford University Press, 1996; first published in 1929).

Sarvepalli Radhakrishnan, president of India from 1962 to 1967, earlier held professorships in Calcutta and Oxford. The Indian philosophical tradition is deep and sophisticated; the Western reader will often come across familiar thoughts and arguments, fascinatingly transformed by the unfamiliar background. Don't panic if you see a few words of Sanskrit.

REFERENCE WORKS

There are now several good one-volume works of this kind: *The Oxford Dictionary of Philosophy*, by Simon Blackburn; *The Oxford Companion to Philosophy*, ed. Ted Honderich; *The Cambridge Dictionary of Philosophy*, ed. Robert Audi (first two Oxford University Press, the last Cambridge University Press).

The best multivolume work in English is (though I say it myself—to understand why I say that, take a close look at the photo at the end of Chapter 8) *The Routledge Encyclopedia of Philosophy*. Not, in most cases, for the individual pocket! This is one to read in a big public library or a university library, or via some such institution which subscribes to the Internet version.

WORKS REFERRED TO IN THE TEXT

CHAPTER 2

Plato, *Crito*. Handy and accessible is *The Last Days of Socrates* (Penguin Books) which contains *The Apology*, *Crito*, and *Phaedo* in a translation by Hugh Tredennick. My only complaint is that the Stephanus numbering is indicated at the top of the page, instead of being given fully in the margin. Should you feel yourself getting keen on Plato a good buy is *Plato: Complete Works*, ed. J. Cooper and D. S. Hutchinson (Hackett Publishing).

CHAPTER 3

David Hume, *Of Miracles*, section X of *An Enquiry Concerning Human Understanding*. Many editions. Try that by L. A. Selby-Bigge (Oxford University Press), which includes Hume's *Enquiry Concerning the Principles of Morals*. Other writings on religion by Hume, also easily available, are his *Dialogues Concerning Natural Religion* and *The Natural History of Religion*.

CHAPTER 4

Anon., *The Questions of King Milinda*, is available in an inexpensive abridged version edited by N. K. G. Mendis (Kandy, Sri Lanka: Buddhist Publication Society, 1993).

Plato, *Phaedrus* 246a ff. and 253d ff. Plato compares the soul to a chariot.

Anon., *Katha Upanishad*, 3. 3–7, 9: the soul is compared to a chariot in the early Indian tradition. An easily available edition of the main Upanishads is in the Oxford University Press World Classics series in a translation by Patrick Olivelle.

CHAPTER 5

Epicurus: The early historian of philosophy Diogenes Laertius wrote a work called *Lives of the Eminent Philosophers*, published in the Loeb Classical Library by Harvard University Press (2 vols.). The last section of volume 2 is devoted entirely to Epicurus, and reproduces some of his writings. (Apart from these only a few fragments have come down to us.)

John Stuart Mill, *Utilitarianism*. This short work, and Mill's *On Liberty* (see below under Chapter 8) can both be found in a volume in the Everyman's Library series published in London by J. M. Dent and Sons and in New York by E. P. Dutton.

Thomas Hobbes, *Leviathan*. One good option is the edition by Richard Tuck published by Cambridge University Press. The famous chapter about the state of nature is Part 1, Chapter 13.

Plato, *Republic* 453–66. Plato's abolition of the family—or should one rather say his introduction of a new, nonbiological concept of the family?—and his reasons for it.

CHAPTER 6

Lucretius, *Of the Nature of Things*, translated by R. E. Latham, introduction by John Godwin, Penguin Books. Lucretius, a Roman of the first century BCE, put the doctrines of Epicurus into Latin verse with the clear intention of converting his compatriots if he could. Godwin's introduction begins: "This book should carry a warning to the reader: it is intended to change your life." The original title is *De rerum natura*.

Berkeley, *Three Dialogues Between Hylas and Philonous*. Numerous editions: a good bet is Roger Woolhouse's edition, published by Penguin Books, which also contains Berkeley's *Principles of Human Knowledge*.

Kant, *Critique of Pure Reason*. Still the best translation is that by Norman Kemp Smith, published by Macmillan. But beginners beware: this is very hard reading.

Sanchez, *Quod nihil scitur*. This is highly specialized stuff, but since I mentioned it in the text I give the details here: edited and translated by Elaine Limbrick and Douglas Thomson, published by Cambridge University Press.

Descartes, *Meditations*. Many editions available. But just in case you find yourself getting interested in Descartes try (in its paperback version) *The Philosophical Writings of Descartes*, translated by J. Cottingham, R. Stoothoff, and D. Murdoch, published by Cambridge University Press (2 vols.). The *Meditations* are in ii. 3–62.

Sextus Empiricus, *Outlines of Pyrrhonism*. Again, this is specialized material. But it would be a pity never to have read at least the first twelve sections of book 1, as far as the point where Sextus explains what the skeptical philosophy is for. R. G. Bury's translation is published in the Loeb Classical Library by Harvard University Press.

CHAPTER 7

Descartes, *Discourse on the Method*. Numerous editions: see the recommendation for Descartes's *Meditations* just above. *The Discourse on the Method* is in i. 111–51. Parts of Descartes's *Treatise on Man* are on pp. 99–108.

Hegel, *Introduction to the Philosophy of History*. An excellent translation is that by H. B. Nisbet and published by Cambridge University Press under the title *Hegel, Lectures on the Philosophy of World History: Introduction*. Pages 25–151 give you all you need.

Charles Darwin, *The Origin of Species*. To be recommended is the edition by J. W. Burrow published by Penguin Books. If you haven't time for the whole of it, at least read chapters 1–4 and 14 (the closing chapter).

Nietzsche, *The Genealogy of Morals*. Translating Nietzsche's resonant and inventive German is a tricky business; that may be why so many English translations are presently available. The two I can recommend are those by W. Kaufmann and R. J. Hollingdale, published by Vintage Books, and by Douglas Smith, published by Oxford University Press in their World Classics series. (But if you *can* comfortably read Nietzsche in German don't even think about reading him in any other language.) The central passage about the activities of the "ascetic priest" is 3. 10–22—but don't limit yourself to that.

CHAPTER 8

John Stuart Mill, *On Liberty*. This and Mill's essay *Utilitarianism* (see above under Chapter 5) are in a volume in the Everyman's Library series published in London by J. M. Dent and Sons and in New York by E. P. Dutton.

John Stuart Mill, *The Subjection of Women*. Available in a volume called *John Stuart Mill: Three Essays*, introduction by Richard Wollheim, published by Oxford University Press; or by itself in a very inexpensive version from Dover Publications.

Anon., *Bṛhadāraṇyaka Upanishad*. As with the *Katha Upanishad* (see above), an accessible edition is Patrick Olivelle's translation of the main Upanishads in the Oxford University Press World Classics series.

Simone de Beauvoir, *The Second Sex*. The translation by H. M. Parshley is one of the most handsome volumes in the Everyman's Library series, published by David Campbell Publishers.

Karl Marx, *Economic and Philosophical Manuscripts*. This is where the quotation in the text comes from. Someone having their first go at Marx should look to some anthology of his writings, perhaps *The Marx–Engels Reader*, ed. R. Tucker, published by Norton. But beware: Marx, especially early Marx, often isn't easy to read—a consequence of habits of thought and style he got from Hegel.

Peter Singer, *Animal Liberation*, is a notable example of a book devoted to the morality of human relationships with animals, published by New York Review Books in 1975. Tom Regan's *The Case for Animal Rights* (University of California Press, 1983) is another.

INDEX

•

Page numbers in *italics* include illustrations and photographs/captions.

PICTURE CREDITS

•

88790; 129: LC-USZ61-259; 130t: LC-USZ62-110411; 130b: LC-USZ62-51570; 136b: LC-USZ62-75102; 139: LC-USZ62-103801; 141: LC-USZ62-69420; 144: LC-DIG-pga-02359; 149: LC-USZ62-116235; 155: LC-USZ62-111675; 157: LC-USZC4-2666; 158: LC-USZ62-51052; 164: LC-USZ62-136363

SHUTTERSTOCK: 16: © Shutterstock/Georgios Kollidas

COURTESY OF WIKIMEDIA COMMONS: 5: Portrait of Chinese Chan-Buddhist monk Wuzhun Shifan/Yorck Project: 10.000 Meisterwerke der Malerei; 6: Bhavacakra (Wheel of Becoming)/Upload by Mistvan; 7: Portrait of Epicurus/Upload by Jastrow; 14: *Liber ethicorum of Henricus de Alemannia*, single leaf, scene: *Henricus de Alemannia in Front of His Pupils*/Yorck Project: 10.000 Meisterwerke der Malerei; 18: Bust of Socrates/Upload by Jastrow; 22: Al-Mubashshir-Manuscript, scene: *Socrates and Two Students*/Yorck Project: 10.000 Meisterwerke der Malerei; 27: Immanuel Kant; 37: Stained-glass window of Creation/Upload by Vassil; 43: The Feeding of the Multitude, *Les très riches heures du duc de Berry*; 45: The resurrection/Upload by Andreas Praefcke; 52: Coin of Menander; 57: Triptolemus and Korē , tondo of a red-figure Attic cup/Upload by Jastrow; 59: Etruscan chariot wheel/Upload by Eric Chan; 61: Statue of Gottfried Wilhelm Leibniz/Upload by Longbow4u; 62: Tibetan prayer wheel/Upload by Agrawal; 69: Buddha enlightening the path/Upload by Sacca; 76: John Michael Wright, Portrait of Thomas Hobbes; 89: René Descartes/Upload by Jean-Charles Guillo; Hendrik ter Brugghen, *Democritus*; 99: Plato in the *Nuremberg Chronicle*; 100: Emanuel Bardou, *Immanuel Kant*/Upload by Andreas Praefcke; 101: Hegel stamp/Scan by NobbiP; 108: Ptolemaic system from J. van Loon, *Harmonia Macroscomica Andreas Cellarius*, 1660–61; 110: Descartes brain section/Digital image by Alexei Kouprianov; 115: Justus Sustermans, *Portrait of Galileo Galilei*; 117: Statue of Søren Kierkegaard/Upload by Christian Bickel; 119: Meissen porcelain figurine of a woman writing/Upload by Andreas Praefcke; 121: The Fall of the Rebel Angels, *Les très riches heures du duc de Berry*; 124: Edward Scriven, *Brutus and the Ghost of Caesar*; 126: *On the Origin of Species*, first-edition title page; 127: Drawing of a stock pigeon; 134: Nietzsche/Scan processed by Anton; 136t: Thomas Henry Huxley, *Evidence as to Man's Place in Nature*; 148: Jan Steen, *The Way You Hear It Is the Way You Sing It (As the Old Sing, So Twitter the Young)*; 151: *Leviathan* title page; 152: Jan Luyken, *Spanish Armada*; 153: Sir Godfrey Kneller, Portrait of John Locke; 165: Two cows in Hyderabad/Upload by Linda